Praise for *Not Made*

"I highly recommend *Not Made for You* to all the women who are in book clubs around the world, or anyone seeking some advice on handling the barriers and struggles for women professionals. I've encountered many of the same stories that Kae outlines. The examples, and the wonderful pieces of advice at the end of each chapter, shouldn't be missed. I found it so helpful and will be passing the book along to those in my mentor circle!"

—LYNNE CAPOZZI, former tech CMO

"A must-read for women in tech—and for the leaders who shape their success. Kae illuminates the barriers too many still face and, more importantly, delivers the strategies to rise above them. This book is a blueprint for empowerment, equipping readers not just to survive but to thrive."

—TALIN ANDONIANS, former tech CEO and board member

"Kae brilliantly exposes how the tech industry's bias forces talented people to waste energy on survival instead of innovation—this book can help us finally change that destructive dynamic."

—JOTHY ROSENBERG, 9x startup founder, executive chairman of Dover Microsystems, and author

"After more than 20 years in tech, I can confirm: You're not imagining it. Kae Kronthaler-Williams offers a candid, compassionate guide that validates your experience while helping you rebuild confidence, reclaim self-worth, and move forward with clarity—minus the fluff."

—KAREN MEYER, customer success executive and former tech CEO

"I know that building a business with heart means embracing the hard work to ensure everyone feels seen, heard, and valued. *Not Made for You* feels like a milestone guidebook for that journey. Kae doesn't just illuminate the realities of bias and discrimination; she gives us the language, the tools, and the unshakeable confidence to navigate and ultimately transform these environments."

—SASHA PURPURA, 2x non-profit CEO

"The chapter on 'Sexism—The Cost of Being Female' deeply resonated with both my personal and professional experiences. I appreciated how it wove together personal stories, peer anecdotes, and research to highlight how sexism shows up in both obvious and subtle ways, often leaving women second-guessing themselves. It examined how bias begins early—shaped by family, education, and social norms—and continues into the workplace through credibility gaps, interruptions, stolen ideas ('hepeating'), unequal pay, exclusion from networks, and stereotypical roles. What stood out most were the practical strategies offered to counter these challenges, from speaking up when credibility is undermined to using humor or assertiveness when interrupted. Overall, the chapter was eye-opening and empowering—raising awareness while providing actionable guidance. It challenges readers not only to recognize sexism but also to address it thoughtfully and support equity in the workplace."

—FRANCHESCA CARRINGTON, senior director of philanthropy for SharkNinja

"Kae's book provides a sobering and unflinching look at the real barriers many women in Tech face, yet manages to be equally optimistic and practical in her advice on how to overcome these hurdles to build a better workplace for us all."

—REGINA LAWLESS, former Meta executive

NOT MADE
FOR
YOU

How Women in Tech Can

Challenge Bias, Claim Their Space, and

Thrive in a System Built for Men

Kae Kronthaler-Williams

RIVER GROVE
BOOKS

Published by River Grove Books
Austin, TX
www.rivergrovebooks.com

Distributed by River Grove Books

Design and composition by Greenleaf Book Group and Sheila Parr
Cover design by Greenleaf Book Group and Sheila Parr
Cover image used under license from Adobe Stock: 908385930 / Xharites

Publisher's Cataloging-in-Publication data is available.

Print ISBN: 978-1-966629-88-7

eBook ISBN: 978-1-966629-89-4

First Edition

Contents

Introduction

"Taking your seat at the table doesn't work so well,
I thought, when no one wants you there."
—Ellen Pao, "This Is How Sexism Works in Silicon Valley"

IT WAS A SITUATION I'd been in many times before. Our executive team members were seated around a conference table, and it was my female colleague's turn to give her presentation.

She stood up and, before she could even finish her first sentence, the male CEO interrupted her. She paused to let him finish, then she resumed her presentation—until he broke in again and started talking over her, sometimes to give his opinions but more often to mansplain the concepts she was already explaining just fine. It was incredibly rude and blatantly disruptive. And it was nothing new to either one of us women in the room that day.

Have you been in a room like that?

Here's another scenario you may recognize. As the only female executive in the company, I led a critical branding and website revamp on a tight deadline. After extensive research—analyzing industry trends, brand messaging, and competitors—I and the NYC design firm I'd hired selected green as our brand color. The executive team reviewed and approved the decision.

Weeks into the design process, an executive called me into his office. He said a male leader on his team, who had previously owned a business, believed the color should be blue. Despite my twenty-plus years in marketing, this was his justification for revisiting the choice. I acknowledged that color is subjective but reaffirmed our research and reminded him that leadership had already signed off on green. Days later, in a meeting with the CEO and other executives, the CEO suddenly suggested we reconsider the brand color—shouldn't it be blue?

And then there are the comments about race. I've experienced firsthand how people can say incredibly biased and racist things without realizing who's in the room. Because my race isn't readily apparent, people often mistake it and say things they probably wouldn't if they knew more about me.

> Bias and racism, sometimes disguised as humor, sometimes as offhand remarks, show up in daily work settings.

One instance occurred during after-dinner drinks with my peers, when a colleague shared a story about their family, mentioning distant relatives who were Black. Another executive responded with what he thought was a funny joke: "Well, if anything ever gets stolen from your family, you will know who the thief is!"

In another setting, a team of us discussed a business partner whose first and last name reflected a Middle Eastern heritage.

Without hesitation, one of the executives said, "Oh, are we going to work with terrorists now?"

Then there was the time I was in a conversation with my CEO and his assistant, talking about a colleague, a dark-skinned man of Indian descent, who had seemed embarrassed during a meeting. As we discussed the situation, the executive assistant casually said, "How could you even tell he was embarrassed? He's so Black." They both laughed.

She was implying that because of his skin color, you couldn't see his embarrassment. In her view, the only way to tell if someone is ashamed or uncomfortable is if their face turns red, which assumes that White skin is the standard for showing emotions.

These moments weren't isolated; they were just a few blatant examples of how bias and racism, sometimes disguised as humor, sometimes as offhand remarks, show up in daily work settings.

It's difficult to know how—or even whether—to respond in situations like these, especially in the workplace. If you speak up, you may temporarily stop the interruptions or the sexist, racist, or otherwise discriminatory comments, but you may also be labeled "overly sensitive" or "difficult to work with" and lose more than you gain. If you stay quiet, grit your teeth, and endure the rude or hurtful behavior—if you "go along to get along"—you might avoid rocking the boat or feel safer in your job. But at what cost to your own integrity? At what cost to your sleep? What kind of culture are you allowing to be passed down to future generations?

These aren't easy questions, but unfortunately, for many of us in primarily minority segments of the US population—women,

> We're fed up and we need solutions.

racial and ethnic minorities, LGBTQ+, the neurodivergent, people with disabilities—they are questions we are forced to grapple with.

For too many years, I have commiserated with colleagues about the abundance of bad behavior in the workplace. I have worked for thirty years in tech, which is well known for its rampant sexism, racism, ageism, and other harmful discriminatory behavior. My colleagues and I are frustrated by the tenor and tone of corporate America. We're fed up and we need solutions.

In these pages I share situations that I and other women have encountered at work, specifically in tech jobs in the United States, though stories like these are common well beyond that industry. I suggest ways you can push back, seek support, or sometimes pause and strategize until you find the right moment for change. While my message works for all workplaces, I especially address the issues faced by women trying to build their careers in the US tech industry.

I wish I'd had a book like this back when I was first starting out or even later in my mid-career, when I finally reached the upper ranks of management, secured a C-suite office, and took my seat at the board-room table. I remember how hard it was to balance my career goals with my desire to speak up against the behaviors I knew were not just rude but were also part of a system built for men, not for women, one that could ultimately hold me back. If you've felt that same struggle, I hope this book offers a way forward—one that helps you build the career you desire and the life you deserve.

Remember the example of my female colleague being interrupted and talked over? There she was, a competent, prepared individual being actively undermined by the CEO. It was awful to witness.

I kept looking at her to let her know I was there for her. I was trying to signal—*Do you want me to jump in here and speak up? Are you going to say something?* But she seemed paralyzed by the intrusions.

She was clearly demoralized, which I could see by her deflated posture as she spoke.

Turns out the CEO wasn't done. Minutes later, while I presented Marketing's quarterly performance, he did the same thing to me! But I was prepared. I refused to back down and instead tried to talk over his cross talk. But he was undeterred and talked right back over me. I doubt anyone learned anything. It was a frustrating meeting for most of us, but for me, I was finally, truly done putting up with it.

After the meeting, my colleague approached me and asked, "What am I doing wrong? Why does everyone speak over me?" She genuinely wanted to find a solution, but she was focused on fixing herself. As I struggled to help her, I began reaching for the pat answers that many of us have been fed for years: "You need to be more commanding when you speak, more definitive in your posture and positions . . ."

But this time I stopped myself. This woman was one of the most intelligent people in the room, and there was no way I was going to feed her the same BS many of us have been made to believe: that's it's somehow *our* fault we're not being perceived as credible or competent, that we are inherently *not as good* as the men in the room, and we need to be more like them. The standard of corporate culture—what is considered acceptable or professional—was shaped by White men and forces everyone else to conform or assimilate to that norm.

Sound familiar? Of course, it's important to acknowledge the great strides we've made in the US workplace. But we need to make even more. We must start by opening our eyes to the realities of our work culture and seeing places where we can force change, even if that's one step or one person at a time. The toxic attitudes in our workplaces are unsustainable. We are stressed out, losing money due to unequal pay, losing promotions we're qualified for, and why? Perhaps those in power, primarily White men, can't bear to lose the power and wealth they hold, and too often they see any kind of power sharing—with women, especially women of color—as defeat. Their biases run deep, and in their minds, people who don't look like them (and think like them) are not to be treated as equals.

Beyond Virtue Signaling—*Real* Change

Over the years, I have offered my experience and advice to others to help them navigate the tech culture, which is known to be male-dominated and rife with issues of misogyny. But I recognized that the problem is too big. My coaching a few individuals will not effect the change that is needed. We all must participate in raising the level of awareness of the discrimination, bias, and harassment we face in the tech industry.

We must continue to beat this drum until lasting change is realized, not the virtue signaling we have seen from some DEI programs. Companies love to make big, public statements about diversity, but too often, there's no real action behind them. True change means taking concrete steps toward building diverse candidate pools and making sure everyone has equal access to opportunities. We need the same concrete, change-oriented approach when it comes to discrimination, bias, and harassment in tech. It's not enough to talk about the problem, we need real steps that make a difference and the follow-through to enforce lasting change. We must force corporate policies that thwart these behaviors. We must demand business cultures that are built to protect us from power-led bias and discrimination—sexism, sexual harassment, and racism—cultures that allow everyone to grow, thrive, and have equal experiences in their careers.

While we do this, we must also help and support each other by sharing our expertise, advising others, or simply being available to listen and provide support.

We must help each other by building networks, sharing job openings, providing referrals, and sharing our wisdom and experience so that we all continue to move up in our careers, get paid based on value, not gender, and access funding for new ventures. I have seen great strides among women over the years as they have moved from competing with one another to actively supporting each other.

I want us to build more support programs to guide us through difficult workplace situations—at least for those you decide are worth sticking with, as you may need to leave those spaces that are just too untenable. With the right tools, you can still thrive in worthy environments despite the prevailing ignorance and bias. I know I have. I want you to as well.

Throughout this book, I arm you with information and tools to help you navigate and address each situation—what to say, when and how to approach a situation, and what legal policies are there to protect you. I share the situations I experienced, what I did, the words I used, the outcomes, and the times I refrained from acting and why. At the end of the book, I provide the principles and strategies I have honed and employed over the past thirty-plus years that have helped me advance from a telemarketer to a CMO.

Looking back, I started my career with so much optimism and ambition. I was excited to see how far I could go within the business world and confident in my ability to make my mark in marketing. I truly love my profession, and I still find it exciting.

Back when I started, I had some awareness that it wouldn't be easy as a woman, let alone a woman of color. My father told me then that I would have to work twice as hard to be considered half as good—a lesson he felt compelled to share as a Black man raising Black daughters in a world stacked against us, a conversation our White counterparts never have to have with their kids. So many of us are told this from an early age. You must dress, speak, and behave "in a certain way" to get ahead. I assumed there would be challenges to contend with, compromises I would need to accept, and obstacles to overcome. I did not realize the nature of these indignities nor how often they would arise. Because the majority don't see these situations as a problem, and the minority needs to overcome them to succeed, the situations, by and large, are left unaddressed.

As a person of color, I have experienced discrimination and prejudice since I was a child. I hoped (and remain hopeful) that in a professional environment, people would be mature and self-aware enough to leave their bias in the office parking lot. Not everyone does. Even now, as a tenured executive with decades in technology, I continue to experience bias.

Many will cite examples of marginalized people who have been successful to reject the notion that there is a systemic problem. Yes, many individuals—of all kinds—have been successful. Relying on edge cases to disprove the experience of the majority of affected people is the definition of a weak argument. I have had a successful career despite widespread bias. Maybe that's the difference—some succeed *despite* this. Imagine how many would thrive without these arbitrary hurdles.

The decades I have spent navigating the professional world have been exhausting. Too often, colleagues have confided their desire just to be *able to do their jobs*. The emotional readiness that one must maintain and the hypervigilance that comes with navigating a shifting landscape are not just taxing but present a real distraction from being the best we can be. Frankly, it wastes time and denies the organization the best results. Corporations that have diverse workgroups outperform others by vast margins. Imagine if every employee felt safe to express their thoughts, not worry about the next slight, and were able to thrive.

> I hope to empower women in tech to navigate challenges, advocate for change, and push for the leadership roles they deserve.

The aim of this book is to explore many forms of bias, from sexism to racism to the everyday microaggressions that too many of us face daily—both within and outside of work. It is both a wake-up call and a call to action. Through real stories, eye-opening data, and practical strategies, I hope to empower women in tech to navigate challenges, advocate for change, and push for the leadership roles they deserve. Whether you've faced discrimination firsthand or want to be part of the solution, this book will equip you with the knowledge and confidence to challenge bias, amplify diverse voices, and help build a more inclusive and equitable workplace. But beyond that, I hope that it helps you build an impactful, joyful career you love while leading a beautiful life.

1

Harsh Reality for Many

"When asked why he didn't invest in women, an investor said this: 'I don't like the way women think. They haven't mastered linear thinking.' He explained further by saying his wife 'could never prioritize her to-do lists properly.'"

—Kathryn Tucker as quoted in *Forbes*

ON FEBRUARY 19, 2017, Susan Fowler published a blog post about her experience at Uber as a site reliability engineer, a position she started in November 2015.[1] As Susan recounts in the post, and has since reiterated in her 2021 book *Whistleblower,* on her first day at Uber, her manager sent her several messages over the company chat. In these messages, he explained that he was in an open relationship and was looking for women with whom he could engage in sex. Susan went to Human Resources (HR) with screenshots of his messages.

In her blog post, Susan shared that she had expectations that HR would step in and put an immediate stop to this. But that's not what happened. Instead, HR concluded that giving him a written warning was the correct response. HR claimed the manager was a "high performer," and they just didn't feel comfortable punishing him for what was conceivably an "innocent mistake."

Susan was told by HR that she could either join another team or remain on his team, but she needed to understand that when review time came around, her manager could give her a poor performance review, and there was nothing HR could do about it. Susan tried to escalate the issue through the chain of command but was told Uber management didn't want to "ruin his career" over a first offense.

Ultimately, she left the team, but within a few months, she learned of other female engineers who'd had similar experiences—several from the same manager. Her experience was clearly not an isolated incident. A group of these victims formed, and members individually approached Uber HR to insist something be done to correct this. But Susan's contact in HR told her the only report they'd received regarding this individual had been hers—something she knew wasn't true. Because of this, Uber would take no further action.

Susan encountered additional inequities at Uber, and as is often the case, her experience was not just about individual misconduct. The harassment, systemic inequality, and HR calamities reflected a broader cultural problem within the company. Like many tech firms, Uber prioritized growth over accountability and ethical practices. By speaking out, Susan forced a high-profile company to look inward and eventually confront the toxic environment it had allowed to persist. Many women face similar challenges in silence, fearing retaliation or career setbacks. Susan showed how a single voice can effect change.

Eventually, Susan left the company. In her blog post, she describes how, before she left, she calculated the number of female engineers in the site reliability engineering teams to be 3 percent.

But her problems were not over. After Susan published her post describing her experience at Uber, she discovered she was being followed—and directly contacted—by private investigators who were known for their work in discrediting victims of sexual misconduct.[2] Misinformation even led to some newspaper reporters claiming that Lyft paid her to write the defamatory blog post to sabotage Uber, their competitor.

Eventually, Uber hired former US Attorney General Eric Holder to investigate its culture, which led to CEO Travis Kalanick stepping down under pressure. His departure represented a watershed moment in Silicon Valley; for the first time, a high-profile, hyper-growth tech company was forced to hold one of its leaders accountable for fostering a toxic culture rather than protect them to ensure continued financial success. It showed how investors and employees demanded that even the most powerful founders could not act with impunity.[3]

Susan Fowler's story is sadly an all too common one. It is perhaps an example of a corporate culture run amok, including an incompetent, or at least indifferent, Human Resources department that failed female employees at every turn. Many of us in marginalized groups—women, ethnic minorities, LGBTQ+, and people with health issues—regularly experience discrimination and bias in the workplace. Studies show that 42 percent of women working in tech report having experienced harassment.[4] That harassment is enough to ruin or at least stall an individual's career, as a second study revealed that 34 percent of employees have left their jobs due to unresolved harassment issues.[5]

These issues are prevalent in a time when women and people of color are already poorly represented in the US tech industry, even as it's booming. But pressure is on to increase these percentages. The 2020 US Census estimates that by 2045, White residents will no longer be the majority.[6] What are now considered minority groups currently fuel US population growth—and they're needed in all aspects of the tech industry and beyond. Employers can't afford to alienate these important members of the future workforce.

Susan's story at Uber includes many elements this book aims to explore: gender discrimination, ignoring or even actively discrediting women who speak out, companies that support violators over the violated, and how this power imbalance continues to victimize many and too often ends up depriving many Americans of the right to earn a living. Clearly our corporate culture has failed to evolve with the changes in our nation's workforce demographics or societal progress.

The Slow March to Progress

Women have contributed economically throughout history, and their numbers in the workforce grew rapidly throughout the twentieth century. During WWII, women made up 34 percent of the workforce.[7] That percentage increased to 43 percent in the 1970s[8] and has risen to 57.5 percent today (2025).[9]

Sex Composition (%) of Total US Workforce, High-Tech Workforce, and All High-Tech Sector Employees 2022[10]

Sex	Total US Workforce	High-Tech Workforce	High-Tech Sector
Male	52.7	77.4	68.1
Female	47.3	22.6	39.1

Note: High-tech workforce comprises workers in science, technology, engineering, and mathematics (STEM) occupations. High-tech sector includes industries comprised of at least 20 percent High-tech workers.

Yet while they make up nearly half of the workforce today, women are vastly underrepresented in leadership and higher paying jobs than are men. Women make up about 22.6 percent of the high-tech workforce and 39.1 percent of the high-tech sector, but they represent just 14 percent of leadership positions within the industry.[11]

Efforts have been made to accommodate the different needs of women and their families—training programs to encourage women in STEM (science, tech, engineering, math) and legislative acts such as the Family and Medical Leave Act, which allows workers to tend to family needs during the workday. But old thinking about gender roles continues to dominate and shape today's corporate culture. This is something Susan—and quite likely you or someone you know—encountered when her company's HR department refused to take her complaints seriously and instead took the side of the offending male employee.

With women workers showing up in greater numbers, carrying education and credentials equal to their male counterparts, or sometimes bearing the burden as their family's sole provider, they are finding themselves on increasingly unequal playing fields. This forces them to choose: Stay quiet so they can keep their jobs and support their families, or speak up and risk losing their jobs and even their careers.

What can we do to level this playing field?

A Rocky Start in My Tech Career

More than thirty years of my life have been spent in software and technology companies. When I started in this industry in the early 1990s, few women—and even fewer people of color—worked in tech. I remember attending a large annual tech conference that had a reputation for employing "booth babes" to entice attendees to enter a vendor's booth.

At that conference, a male coworker tried to talk me into working in the "front of the booth" to attract men so we could sell our company's wares. He suggested that my looks would help attract men and, in turn, sell our solutions. I was young at the time, and while his comment embarrassed and angered me, I didn't feel I had a choice. He was senior to me. I remember feeling stunned and uncomfortable by the suggestion, realizing that he valued my appearance rather than my intellect, skills, or experience. I was numb for the rest of the day. It was a moment of realization of how I was being perceived, and it planted a seed of frustration that would grow into an awareness of the barriers I and other women face in the workplace.

> I remember feeling stunned and uncomfortable by the suggestion, realizing that he valued my appearance rather than my intellect, skills, or experience.

At this show, one of my tasks was to ask questions of prospective customers in order to gauge how serious they were about our products. I recall asking one prospective customer why he was attending the show. His answer? "To find a wife." I laughed it off, assuming it was a joke. He insisted he was serious—and then asked if I was interested.

Later, coworkers told me about a different customer who'd been trying to find out which hotel I was staying at. He'd told me earlier he thought I was "cute as a button" and he wanted to fly me up to his cabin in Colorado. He was the same customer who, months later, when a coworker and I were attending a business dinner with him, asked my male coworker if I was his wife or girlfriend.

Years later, when I returned to work at this show, a woman asked me where I was from. I replied, "Massachusetts." She responded, "No, what island are you from? You're so exotic." I think she meant non-White.

The company where I worked at the time was established in a small town in Massachusetts. Most of the employees, including me, lived in the surrounding towns. I grew up in a predominantly White area, often the only Black kid in my class. These racial ratios were, not surprisingly, reflected in the employee population.

The Sexist Mentor

I worked there for about nine years, starting my career as a telemarketer, advancing to a marketing assistant, then to senior marketing manager with a group of three direct reports. I wanted to get to the next level within the company as a director. My boss at the time (whom I adored) took an interest in my career. He had studied theology and was very bright. He liked to go for walks, either down to the cafe for coffee or outside the building if the weather was nice. He would sometimes invite me and use these walks to ask about my career aspirations and to coach me about leadership and business. I appreciated these conversations and his willingness to take the time out of his day to give me one-on-one coaching.

During one of these walks, he suggested I might benefit from some mentorship from one of the executives. He was trying to give me greater visibility at the executive level. He arranged a meeting with my new mentor, the VP of Human Resources, and invited me to an executive staff meeting to present some programs I worked on.

Imagine how excited I was for this opportunity. I was in my late twenties and ambitious. I had set my sights on climbing the corporate ladder. I knew then that I wanted to be an executive at a technology company. I'd shared my ambitions with my mother, who encouraged me to work hard to achieve the goals I had set for myself.

The day came for the executive presentation. Naturally, I was a little nervous. There was a new CEO, and it was my first time in a room full of executives. One other woman may have been in the room. When it was my turn to present, the CEO kindly asked me a question. He tried to make me comfortable and appear interested in my presentation. I answered. I did a decent job presenting and holding up my end of the conversation. I was happy with myself for overcoming my nerves and performing well.

After the executive staff meeting, I met with my new mentor, the VP of HR. He accused me of lying when I answered the CEO's question. I told him that I had not lied. I don't remember the question, but I do remember thinking there was no reason to lie about my answer. It wasn't a right or wrong answer. I stated again that I did not lie. He said yes, you did; I could tell. Then he said, "You know what you need to do? You need to smile more. You have a nice smile."

Snapshot of Women and Minorities in US Tech

These experiences happened in the 1990s, and I know I wasn't alone. Women were terribly underrepresented, and when we did take a seat at the table, we were often mistaken for girlfriends, told to smile more, and generally not taken seriously.

While the tech industry has evolved, the underrepresentation of women and minorities remains a significant issue. Many of the issues I experienced early in my career still persist. Just remember the case of Susan Fowler at Uber, which happened in 2017. Her case is a stark reminder that situations of unequal treatment are far from relics of the past. Women and minorities continue to face systemic barriers, and we are disproportionately underrepresented in tech.

Delving into the technology industry demographics paints a clearer picture of how much work remains to achieve true equity and inclusion. Have we made any real progress? Where are we in terms of bias and discrimination in the corporate world? How about in the field of tech? We've seen statistics for the overall US workforce, but now let's delve into technology industry demographics.

There are approximately 5.2 million tech workers in the US as of 2022. White workers make up 62.6 percent of the high-tech sector workforce, followed by Asian workers (16.9 percent), Hispanic and Latino workers (9.5 percent), and Black workers (7.6 percent).[12] These figures are shown in the following chart. Minorities, especially Hispanic and Black workers, are significantly sparse in the high-tech workforce. This also holds true at the manager level, where Asian workers make up 15.3 percent, Hispanic and Latino workers 8.1 percent, and Black workers 5.7 percent.[13]

Race/Ethnic Composition (%) of Total US Workforce, High-Tech Workforce, and All High-Tech Sector Employees 2022

Race/Ethnicity	Total US Workforce	High-Tech Workforce	High-Tech Sector
Asian	6.5	18.1	16.9
Black	11.6	7.4	7.6
Hispanic	18.7	9.9	9.5
Other	4.8	4.8	3.4
White	58.4	59.9	62.6

High-tech jobs tend to be higher paid and relatively more stable than other non-technical occupations. The Bureau of Labor Statistics reported that, in 2023, the median annual wage for technology-related occupations was $101,650 compared to $48,060 for the total US workforce.[14] The point of all of this data is that this is where the money is, yet compared to their White peers, women and minorities are significantly underrepresented.

In leadership, representation is even worse. Women constituted 28 percent of tech professionals but only 14 percent of tech leaders in 2023. But there is some good news. Since 2015, the number of women at the C-suite level has increased from 17 to 28 percent, and the number of women at the vice president and senior vice president levels has also seen significant improvement.[15]

The biggest problem lies in the pipeline for future growth. In 2023, only 3 and 4 percent of women were promoted at the manager and director levels. All women lose ground in the middle of the pipeline, which is where we find directors and managers. Progress for women of color lags behind their peers in every pipeline stage. If this inequity isn't addressed, women of color will remain severely underrepresented in leadership positions—and almost nonexistent in the C-suite.

The 2023 Women Who Tech report anonymously surveyed 930 tech employees, founders, and investors globally on their experiences in the tech sector. It looked at barriers people face in the tech and startup industry. Despite tech companies' greater focus on diversity and inclusion initiatives and pledges, the impact of high-profile harassment lawsuits, and the global impact of the #MeToo movement, women—especially women of color—are still experiencing roadblocks.[16]

Women-Led Companies

And what about starting our own companies? It seems the logical answer. If we can't progress our careers in tech companies—run and staffed primarily by White males—then let's start our own companies and foster our own opportunities!

Examining the funding data, we find a similar lack of support and resources for women-owned businesses. In 2023, female-led tech companies in the US made up 13.2 percent of the total, down from 15.1 percent in 2022. Over the past several years, men have outnumbered women among new startup founders by nearly six to one.[17] While many say this is a pipeline issue, when you look into funding, you may find other reasons for the small percentage of female-led companies.

In 2022, only 2.1 percent of venture capital investments in the US went to businesses founded solely by women. This marked the lowest percentage of venture capital allocated since 2016.[18] Female founders who raised money alongside male cofounders experienced a significant increase, raising 26.1 percent of all venture capital, up from 18.2 percent the previous year. This suggests the investment community has a long way to go in addressing its bias toward female-founded companies.[19]

For Black women founders, funding is even a greater issue. Black women business owners who apply for funding have a rejection rate that is three times higher than that of White business owners.[20]

Lack of funding isn't the only issue for female founders. They, like other female tech workers, experience a high percentage of discrimination and harassment. Among women founders, 57 percent said they have been discriminated against in the last twelve months.[21] Fully half—50 percent—of women founders who have been harassed experienced sexual harassment (unwanted sexual advances, derogatory comments about sex, etc.). While more than half—65 percent—of women founders report they were told by male investors that they would be able to raise more money if they were men.

Research also shows that female founders are asked more about potential risks and losses during the pitch process than male founders, who are often asked about gains and achievements. This same report provided insight into investors' thoughts. More than one third—36 percent—of investors surveyed claimed the lack of investment in startups led by females or members of underrepresented groups has more to do with the pipeline and lack of deal flow within these demographics; they did not acknowledge any bias against women.[22]

The double standard in funding and mentorship for entrepreneurs is often subtle, but it's unmistakable. One female entrepreneur I spoke with shared her experience at a startup accelerator, where the questions she faced included her personal status. Here is what she said.

At a three-month accelerator for startups, we had to attend a "mentor matching" event where we had about three to five minutes to meet with each mentor, and they asked us questions about our business, and we were allowed to ask them about their experience in the business world. I was personally asked if I was married and if I had children. Later, when the program facilitators were evaluating our experience, all of the female entrepreneurs shared their frustrations with being asked questions about their marital status, if they had children, and how they think they could balance family life and responsibilities with starting and growing a business. Our male counterparts were actually shocked because none of them were asked the same questions.[23]

Is this a problem? Of course it is. If a person isn't aware of their bias or refuses to admit to it, then they can't fix it.

Yet we frequently read about Silicon Valley doing its best to include women and people of color. A whopping 72 percent of venture capitalists report that they prioritize DEI practices to help underrepresented groups, including women.[24] However, 40 percent of women tech startup founders say investors have harassed them, and 65 percent were propositioned for sex![25]

Clearly investors still don't see that there is an equity issue, nor do they acknowledge what is clearly widespread harassment of female founders.

The Ugly Gender Problem Illustrated

Consider the story of Kathryn Minshew, owner of career-development platform The Muse, initially reported by Issie Lapowsky in her 2014 *Wired* magazine article "This Is What Tech's Ugly Gender Problem Really Looks Like."[26]

While searching for fundraising for her company, Kathryn Minshew met an investor who was the guest of honor at a dinner hosted by a young tech entrepreneur group. The investor approached Minshew about meeting for dinner as he was interested in her company. On that day, he changed the location of their meeting to a bar in his hotel, claiming a change in his schedule. Kathryn was uneasy about the change but went ahead, as she had initially scheduled the meeting with his assistant, so she thought the meeting was legitimately about business.

According to Minshew, the meeting was typical until the investor asked her to move to a couch, sat down very close to her, touched her body, and put his arm on her back during their conversation, which turned personal. When she tried to return the conversation to business, to no avail, and had to "push his chest off of her," she got up and left.

Kathryn Tucker, founder of RedRover, a social event discovery platform, pitched her idea to an investor at a New York tech event. When she finished, the investor said he didn't invest in women. Kathryn asked why. His response: "I don't like the way women think. They haven't mastered linear thinking." [27]

So, what does all this mean for female founders and the investment community? There are still significant hurdles for the investment community regarding female founders. Investors' biases—conscious or otherwise—influence their decisions on investing in women in tech, including that they are not technically competent and cannot lead and grow successful companies. There is still the view that a successful entrepreneur is male and that women-owned businesses are much riskier.

We are still contending with male-dominated networks, which is true in the investment community. Women, especially women of color, need access to the same networks, mentorship opportunities, and resources as men. We need more representation in the investment community and more females and people of color in venture capital firms who will not hold these biases and stereotypes.

This illustrates the bias faced by female founders. Women are often subjected to greater skepticism rooted in gender bias and stereotypes about their abilities and expertise, and it undermines their credibility and limits their opportunities to start and build companies.

Why is this bias and discrimination of female workers happening in tech? Considered to be the most progressive, highly educated group, this industry and the people who join it should be more self-aware. Still, if you look at representation across tech versus all US occupations, you will find that women and minorities are under-represented. Women comprise 26 percent of the tech industry versus 49 percent across all occupations. Similarly, Black or African American people represent 8 percent in tech compared to 12 percent in all occupations, and Hispanic or Latino individuals are 8 percent in tech versus 17 percent in all occupations.[28]

Diverse Teams Make Better Decisions

The argument for more diversity is rooted in studies that have shown that diverse groups make better decisions and that companies with diverse workforces are more successful than those with homogeneous workforces.

Diverse workgroups bring new ideas and perspectives to decision-making, but this is not the only benefit. In research conducted by Katherine Phillips at Kellogg School of Management, she found that socially different groups outperform homogenous groups not because of the new ideas they bring but because the diversity in the group creates awkwardness and, in turn, the need to diffuse the tension, which leads to better group dynamics and better problem-solving.[29]

In 2017, Forbes's research on inclusive decision-making showed that inclusive—meaning diverse—teams make better business decisions a stellar 87 percent of the time. Their Cloverpop study found that "inclusive decision making drives better company performance and gives a decisive competitive advantage . . . Business teams drive decision making twice as fast with half the meetings. Decision outcomes can improve by 60 percent."[30]

This efficiency also leads to an increase in the company's bottom line, as financial performance improved among those companies with more diverse teams making corporate decisions.[31]

More diversity in companies also forces internal change. I have experienced this firsthand. At a recent company, we had four women and three men on the executive staff—more women than men for the first time in my leadership experience. I have noticed that because there isn't only one woman in the room, who could be easily ignored, men are forced to interact with us. Having diverse work groups forces people to work together and consider others' opinions and ideas. The hope is that they will start to recognize that *everyone* is worthy of being in that room, at that table, and making sound business decisions; and the research proves that.

These examples—and countless others—show us that while the US demographics have shifted in many ways, American high-tech is not keeping pace. Women and people of color are still being discriminated against at work. We are working in conditions that require us to shift our behavior to survive, never mind our desire to also thrive.

Women are navigating a system never designed with their success in mind—a system built by men, for men. This male-dominated environment is apparent in everything from hiring practices that favor male networks to performance reviews that praise assertiveness in men but criticize it in women.

Women are often excluded from situations where informal decisions are made, such as after-work events, golf outings, or hallway conversations. These casual gatherings often turn into business discussions, leaving women out of opportunities and denying them the influence that comes from those conversations. In tech, leadership and communication style preferences lean toward what works for men, forcing women to carefully balance being confident without being seen as pushy, and to perform their jobs with competence without being labeled too ambitious.

Bias is also embedded in workplace benefits and cultural norms, from parental leave policies that assume women are primary caregivers to rigid work hours that ignore the realities of school drop-offs, sick kids, and other caregiving responsibilities that disproportionately fall to women. This system makes women work harder to prove themselves in an environment that doubts their place from the start. Recognizing that this system wasn't built for you is the first step in navigating, challenging, and transforming it to create a successful career.

> Recognizing that this system wasn't built for you is the first step in navigating, challenging, and transforming it to create a successful career.

While Chapter 1 highlights the obstacles women face in the workplace, Chapter 2 supports you on the next step in the process by providing the critical language needed to identify and address these issues. We'll explore the lexicon of discrimination—covering sexism, sexual harassment, ageism, racism, and microaggressions—while diving into Ellen Pao's story as a case study. By the end of the book, you'll have a solid foundation to recognize, name, and challenge the biases that shape workplace dynamics, setting the stage for meaningful change.

CLOSING THOUGHTS

Corporate America is not keeping pace with US demographics. Women and people of color continue to face systemic barriers that limit their rise to leadership. Progress remains slow despite research showing that diverse teams make better decisions.

- **Women and people of color remain underrepresented in tech.** This is especially true in leadership and executive roles.

- **Bias against female founders seeking investment hinders their success.**

- **Systemic bias is common.** Cases like Susan Fowler's and Kathryn Minshew's highlight the career roadblocks caused by systemic bias.

- **Despite evidence that diverse teams outperform homogeneous ones, inclusion remains a challenge.** The US tech industry is built by men, for men, with biases in hiring, decision-making, and leadership. Recognizing this is the first step in navigating and transforming it to build a successful career.

2

Discrimination and Bias— Who's In, Who's Out

"The issue is that we are staying in condos, and I was thinking that gents wouldn't mind sharing, but gals might. Why don't we punt on her and find two guys who are awesome. We can add 4–8 women next year."

—Chi-Hua Chien, then senior partner at
Kleiner Perkins, quoted in Re/code

IN 2007, ELLEN PAO became a junior partner at Kleiner Perkins, the venture capital firm where she had worked since 2005. Five years after she became partner, in 2012, she filed a gender discrimination lawsuit against the firm.[1] Pao described a workplace teeming with gender discrimination and harassment. She detailed instances of being overlooked for promotions, having her ideas dismissed in meetings, and feeling a lack of support when she reported sexual harassment to a senior partner, as the company did not have an HR department at the time.

She specifically highlighted her experience with Ajit Nazre, a partner at the firm, who allegedly, after she ended a sexual relationship with him, retaliated against her by excluding her from important meetings and emails. Nazre received minimal disciplinary action, including a deduction of $22,000 from his pay, until outside investigations revealed multiple instances of harassment.[2]

Pao Breaks Her Silence and Sues

In May 2012, Ellen Pao had had enough. She sued Kleiner Perkins for gender discrimination, alleging she was denied promotions and was ultimately being fired because she raised concerns about sexual harassment. In her complaint, Pao cited, among other inequities, receiving unequal treatment in investment opportunities, compensation, and board seat nominations compared to her male counterparts, despite her contribution to the firm's ventures—including the very successful RPX Corporation.

Pao's attorneys argued that the company ignored or openly rejected Pao's contributions, and pointed to one early recommendation, in 2008, that the venture capital firm invest in a young company called Twitter. Pao had met with Twitter CEO Jack Dorsey and felt the company had real promise. Instead, senior partners rejected the idea, with one suggesting such a company would not survive.[3] Twitter and other companies Pao recommended would later be considered valuable investments, even though many that were recommended by the men who were promoted above her were not.

On the stand in her lawsuit, Pao shared instances that further supported the existence of a discriminatory environment at Kleiner Perkins, including a Valentine's Day gift that she considered inappropriate, multiple conversations in a company jet that she felt objectified women, being excluded (as were all women) from a dinner party in Al Gore's apartment, and missing out on a company ski trip, again where no women were invited.

I'm sure many of us can relate to Pao's reaction, which was to not speak out about these instances when they occurred simply because she didn't want a reputation as a complainer.

Let's return to the Chi-Hua Chien quote that opened this chapter. His experience and behavior, as revealed in the trial, showcased the double standards and gender discrimination women often face. Chien was a senior partner at Kleiner Perkins. He has MS and MBA degrees from Stanford. Ellen Pao has degrees from Princeton and Harvard. In Ellen's reviews, coworkers described her as territorial, difficult, harsh, and demanding credit—all cited as factors in her termination. Similar language was used in Chien's reviews, yet he was promoted.

Chien was asked about the investments he brought to the firm and their performance. Had any of them been successful—i.e., gone public or sold? They had not.

Pao sent Chien emails about being excluded. Chien responded and forwarded his commentary to other partners: "This constant Ellen bullshit really pisses me off." His response to Ellen when she shared in an email that she felt left out: "It bothers me when you are territorial and turn things into an issue of ownership/credit." He forwarded an email to other partners that Ellen wrote about a meeting with companies getting funding from Y Combinator— a prestigious startup accelerator based in Silicon Valley that offers seed funding, mentorships, and resources to early-stage startups in exchange for equity—in which he wrote: "This is stupid shit. Why is she always positioning when I'm just trying to help the partnership source?"[4]

Ellen wasn't the only person who had an issue with Chien's behavior. Another female colleague complained that getting Chien to review another company with her was difficult. The company required that you get consensus from other partners.

The defense presented a different view of the Chien-Pao relationship, showing earlier emails in which Chien tried including Ellen in meetings with startups and partnership discussions. Chien explained the Al Gore dinner by stating that only ten people could fit in Al Gore's living room, and only three were affiliated with Kleiner Perkins. As for the all-male ski trip, Chien said he invited a female colleague, but she couldn't make it.[5]

Ultimately, Ellen Pao lost. The jury delivered split verdicts on all counts, with the final outcome favoring Kleiner Perkins. Two jurors discussed their votes, and one of them, Marshallette Ramsey, supported Ellen Pao. She encouraged other women to stand up for themselves. She said, "It seemed that the men, with the same character flaws that Ellen was cited with, were able to propel and continue." Steve Sammut wasn't convinced that Ellen experienced gender discrimination, but he hoped that Kleiner Perkins would still be punished for how it generally treated employees.[6]

You may be wondering why a case in which a woman who felt discriminated against sued—but lost—is worth examining. I wanted to share this case for two reasons. First, it is a crystalline example of how double standards work against many women in the workplace, especially in tech. The second reason this is noteworthy is what happened after the case concluded. Let's take a closer look at these.

One Rule for Them; Another Rule for Us

Decisive and authoritative men are typically considered competent and demonstrate laudable leadership qualities. Women who display the same behavior are frequently labeled as bossy, abrasive, and, of course, my favorite one—a bitch. Not collaborative, not capable. When a man tries to climb the corporate ladder, he is considered confident and ambitious. When a woman strives for growth within her career, she is construed as pushy, self-consumed, and aggressive.

Assertive women may make people uncomfortable because they are seen as not playing the traditional gender role. Men who speak up in meetings are viewed as contributing and showing excellent leadership potential. When women do that, we are frequently considered opinionated, and the value of our ideas is often questioned, denigrated, or unrecognized—just like the colleague I described at the beginning of the book, who was talked over and mansplained by the male CEO (who then did the same thing when it was my turn!).

How often have you conveyed an idea in a meeting only to receive a tilt of the head that shows doubt, and then they move on to ask the men in the room what they think about it? This has happened to me—or in front of me—countless times. When a man confronts someone directly, they are viewed as displaying leadership qualities: being assertive and decisive. When a woman, let alone a woman of color, confronts a conflict directly, they are viewed as intimidating, confrontational, or "emotional."

Chi-Hua Chien and Ellen Pao had similar styles at Kleiner Perkins, detailed in their performance reviews that were made public in the courtroom. But their outcomes were quite different: Chien got promoted; Pao got fired.

The Pao Effect

Should Ellen Pao have kept quiet? Should she not have taken her case to the courts? Should she have taken the settlements that were offered?

She was offered money in exchange for her silence. Kleiner attempted to settle three times. One figure was between three and five million dollars. After the trial, she turned down a $2.7 million payment from Kleiner as it required her to sign a non-disparagement clause.[7] What she did instead was to continue speaking out about her case and the wider issues of discrimination within her industry.

This has become known as the "Pao Effect"—and it has shaken up the tech industry. It encouraged more women and underrepresented groups to speak up and push for systemic changes. After Ellen Pao, several other suits were filed in Silicon Valley. According to the Department of Fair Employment and Housing, sex discrimination complaints from all industries filed with California's civil rights agency increased 61 percent from 2011 to 2014.[8]

More Women Come Forward

One of these cases, part of the "Pao Effect," originated in Microsoft headquarters. In September 2015, Katie Moussouris filed suit against Microsoft.[9] She charged that the company discriminated against her and other female workers because of their gender. She stated that she was passed over for more than one promotion while less-qualified male colleagues were promoted.

Moussouris claimed that the numerical ranking system Microsoft used at the time to evaluate, compensate, and promote employees was unfair to women. According to the lawsuit, female technical workers typically received lower scores than male peers as the rankings were biased against them.

Moussouris also stated that she complained about a higher-up who was sexually harassing female colleagues. According to Moussouris, Microsoft found the allegations to have merit but merely reassigned the person to a different position. Moussouris claimed he retaliated by giving her a low bonus and diminishing her responsibilities.

Microsoft's workforce was 76 percent male at the time, and at the executive level, it was 88 percent male.[10]

Lower Levels Also Speak Out

Discrimination isn't confined to a specific level or position within an organization. No matter what level you are at now or in the future, you could face bias and prejudice. I have faced discrimination from entry to executive levels. Here are a few examples of mid- and lower-level employees facing gender and race discrimination. Most of these companies are well known in the US, though the lawsuits and outcomes are not.

In 2015, Chia Hong, a program manager at Facebook (now Meta), sued for sex and race discrimination. She claimed that Facebook was a hostile work environment and that she'd been ordered to organize parties and serve drinks to male colleagues. Her male colleagues were never required to do this. She claimed her boss referred to her as an "order taker" and either ignored or belittled her input in settings where she was the only woman in the room. Her boss asked her why she didn't just stay home and care for her children. She claimed coworkers excluded her because she was the only person of Chinese descent on her team. Hong dropped the case after it went to mediation. It was not disclosed if there was a settlement.[11]

In March 2015, Tina Huang, an engineer at Twitter (now X), sued the company for gender discrimination. She cited lack of formal procedures for granting promotions, revealing that managers had complete discretion over whether software engineers were promoted. Those decisions, she contended, were tainted with prejudice and gender-based stereotypes, and therefore, few female employees advanced to senior leadership positions.

Huang and her lawyers attempted a civil class action lawsuit involving 135 female software engineers. They were denied the class action suit when Superior Court Judge Mary Wiss ruled that, by itself, disparate impact—when a neutral policy or practice negatively affects a specific group of people based on a protected characteristic such as gender or race—wasn't enough to allow a class to form. She pointed to the US Supreme Court's 2011 decision *Walmart Stores v. Dukes*. The ruling made it more difficult for plaintiffs to get class actions certified. Disparate (individual) impact alone is insufficient for a class to form.[12]

All of this occurred in a company that was overwhelmingly male. According to company records, 70 percent of Twitter employees were male. In leadership and technical roles, women comprised just 21 percent of leadership and 10 percent of leaders in technical jobs.[13] These statistics highlight the ongoing gender disparity in tech leadership. What is known as the "feedback loop" of hiring like-for-like, where men are more likely to hire other men, contributes to the lack of female representation in leadership and technical roles. This disparity reflects a broader pattern where women are relegated to non-technical or supportive roles, limiting their opportunities for advancement.

Then there was Adrienne Williams, a Black female salesperson at Oracle who filed a lawsuit in 2017 alleging Oracle engaged in pay discrimination based on race and gender. Her case was part of a broader issue at Oracle for gender and race discrimination that led to federal investigations into the company's pay practices.[14] Ultimately, Oracle agreed to pay $25 million to resolve a class action lawsuit alleging pay discrimination against four thousand female employees in California. That $25 million was a small price to pay for Oracle and only amounted to one or two paychecks for most of the women.[15] Oracle also agreed to establish measures to comply with equal pay laws.[16]

More recent cases include one in 2020 where two Black female former employees, Ifeoma Ozoma and Aerica Shimizu Banks, accused Pinterest of gender and racial discrimination, alleging they were underpaid and retaliated against for speaking out.[17]

In 2021, Owen Diaz, a Black former employee of Tesla's Fremont factory, won a racial harassment lawsuit for facing frequent racial slurs and a hostile work environment. Diaz was awarded $15 million. This was followed by a lawsuit in 2022 by a female production associate who sued for pervasive sexual harassment, where she described a culture of sexual comments, unwanted touching, and retaliation after she reported harassment. Her lawsuit contributed to many discrimination and harassment cases against Tesla and increased pressure on the company to address its workplace culture.[18]

In 2021, Google faced racial discrimination claims by several Black employees who alleged a culture of racial discrimination that resulted in being unfairly paid, blocked from promotions, and treated unequally. A lawsuit was filed in 2022 against Google, echoing these complaints and accusing the company of systemic racial bias. Google has since faced criticism for its issues with diversity and inclusion.[19]

Not everyone in these cases won a lawsuit or settlement, of course, but like Ellen Pao, these women spoke up regardless of what the outcome would be. These women refused to tolerate the status quo and were emboldened to speak up about the unspoken, giving voice to the hidden and insidious acts of discrimination and bias they face in the workplace.

> These women refused to tolerate the status quo and were emboldened to speak up about the unspoken. Their actions forced a very public reckoning in Silicon Valley, not unlike the #MeToo movement that targeted the entertainment industry.

Their actions—their bravery—forced a very public reckoning in Silicon Valley, not unlike the #MeToo movement that targeted the entertainment industry. What did both of these movements show us? That real change often comes at a cost. Sometimes, it takes individuals putting their careers and reputations on the line to raise awareness and drive significant change.

Recognizing Our Biases

According to Freada Kapor Klein, founder of the Level Playing Field Institute and partner with Kapor Capital, more than a dozen venture capital firms and technology companies approached Ellen Pao and asked her to help combat gender bias in their companies.[20] This is a significant point to highlight. By speaking out and not backing down for a payout, Pao brought to the forefront issues that are often tolerated, brushed aside, or worse, concealed. Her actions raised her profile, and she is helping progressive companies take a critical lens to their own cultures and practices.

This is the progress we need. We all must do our part to bring awareness to these issues, or the corporate culture filled with bias and discrimination won't change.

These cases also show how difficult it is to prove bias, as it is often implicit, pervasive, and generally accepted. We all have biases, sometimes subtle, where our innate preferences drive our decision-making, and we have unconscious biases, which we're not even aware of. These biases can have a snowball effect; we hire people who look like us, are "like us," or are people we want to be like. This is why ageism, racism, and sexism prevail in corporate environments and the world at large.

One example of an unconscious bias is how our society gravitates toward beautiful people. We see it in our personal lives. Media paints a picture of what is considered attractive, and we all conform to that notion. We gravitate toward people who have what are deemed beautiful features, and we want those features ourselves. This can include height, weight, accent, and skin color.

If we are unaware of our innate biases and how they influence our decision-making, we may end up creating environments and business practices that foster discrimination and lack diversity. We see this prevail in corporate America and the tech industry. Look around you. Do you see a diverse group of people at every level in your company? And I don't mean one or two women or people of color. I mean a genuinely diverse culture at every level.

Another consideration with bias is the degree to which it must be offensive before it is deemed discriminatory or the degree to which it creates or contributes to a hostile work environment. Too often, when issues are raised with a manager, the result is a shrug of the shoulders accompanied by a "Well, I'm sure they didn't mean it that way." Sound familiar? Let's face it; in the case of Susan Fowler and Katie Moussouris, the men who were sexually harassing them were not fired or demoted; they merely got what equates to a slap on the wrist, and Oracle's $25 million settlement meant an extra one or two paychecks for the people impacted.

Discrimination Takes an Emotional Toll

This imbalance takes a toll on our emotional state at work. I don't know about you, but I am always waiting for the next verbal slight, the next case of unequal treatment, the next transgression because of my gender or race.

I wasn't always consciously aware of how much this affected me, nor that I was in a state of perpetual hypervigilance. That realization came when I was on an executive team where I wasn't the only female. For the first time, I could discuss these situations, giving voice to the experience and finding validation in knowing I wasn't the only one. Talk about waiting to exhale!

I don't know what is worse when it comes to being on the receiving end of discrimination and harassment: waiting for it to happen or watching it happen. There is always a hesitation—wait, did that happen? Did I hear that correctly? And then the adrenaline, fast heartbeat, and loud drumming in your ears. The world stops; you are stunned, doubting yourself, angry, trying to decide if you should respond, if it's even safe to respond . . . all simultaneously. You are embarrassed and humiliated. Whether you respond or not, you reel for hours or even days. It requires immense emotional labor.

You now feel alienated, like you don't belong here. You don't feel a part of the company; that feeling extends to your team—even if they weren't in the room. You don't trust anyone, especially if there isn't anyone in the company who looks like you. You dread coming to work the next day and the day after that. You lose interest in your role, you lose loyalty to the company, and if it continues to happen, you leave your job.

What can we do to prevent these acts of discrimination and make our workplaces safe for everyone?

Understanding the different types of discrimination so you can recognize them when they occur and speaking up for yourself and others when it happens are critical to building awareness of discriminatory or biased acts and squelching them. Unless warranted, it doesn't have to be as big as a class action lawsuit, but if we don't address these issues and voice how we're affected, we won't ever change the status quo. We won't ever be able to come to work with our guard down. We won't ever be able to feel fully present and perform at our highest level. We must force awareness, no matter how uncomfortable it is for us and them.

As we've seen in the case of Ellen Pao, change doesn't happen overnight. But bringing awareness to these issues is the right start. The fight for greater parity and equal rights for all, not just the privileged few, requires a constant focus on education and awareness, and for all of us to step up, speak out, and support each other.

The more we show up, the further the movement will reach. We saw this happen with the #MeToo movement, and we saw it in 2020, after the murder of George Floyd at the hands of the Minneapolis police, when the Black Lives Matter (BLM) movement gained strength and people moved beyond individual posts on social media and actually took to the streets.

And we saw the far reach of a movement in January 2017, when people showed up to the women's march in Washington, DC—and at sister marches around the world—to spread a pro-human-rights agenda and to protest the harmful policies promised by newly elected Donald Trump (what would be his first term). I marched on that day in Boston, and I noticed that there was a shift in this fight. This time, many men—young and old—were there with their partners. And we saw this happen not only across the US but worldwide—London, Sydney, New Delhi, Mexico City, Argentina, Antarctica, to name a few.[21] People were making their voices heard, speaking up for the kind of world they wanted for themselves and their children. We saw this with Ellen Pao and "The Pao Effect"; after Ellen Pao spoke out, others felt emboldened to do the same.

We have made and continue to make progress. But we must continue to speak up and drive awareness. As these movements showed, change doesn't happen overnight, nor does it guarantee it will stick. Look at DEI (diversity, equity, and inclusion) efforts in business. In the wake of the BLM movement, many corporations initiated DEI programs. But now, only a few years later, we see that this was—in far too many cases—merely "virtue signaling" rather than true dedication to what DEI stands for. Many corporations are now backing away from these programs or shuttering them entirely.

What can we do as companies back away from their diversity commitments? We must continue to speak up and fight for corporate programs that mandate safe and equitable work environments for all women, incorporating bias and microaggression training and inclusivity in promotion processes.

Corporations must provide training and skill-building so that everyone has a chance to succeed regardless of their backgrounds, education, or networks. We must continue fighting for policy changes to effect equal pay and supplemental childcare; we must advocate for ourselves. We as individuals need to take action by ensuring equal access in our hiring practices, challenging bias in everyday interactions, and supporting underrepresented colleagues in their career growth.

Let's acknowledge that it is unfair that the very people who are on the receiving end of discrimination and bias are also burdened with having to call it out and deal with it. But this burden is necessary to take on if we are to champion our rights and to advocate for change.

If you are experiencing any degree of sexism or racial bias, speak to your HR department to let them know you experienced a serious issue within your workplace. Look for opportunities to suggest training that might benefit your corporate culture. Throughout the following chapters, I share ways to productively approach these topics and suggest methods to address sexism, sexual harassment, racism, and ageism as they happen.

Start with a Common Language: Types of Discrimination

In the hopes of arming you with information and suggested strategies to survive and thrive in your work environments, building a foundation of understanding and language is important. Language plays a powerful role in our communication and interactions. A firm grasp of the vocabulary and terminology will prepare you to navigate conversations and workplace dynamics more easily, offering a better chance for positive outcomes.

You need to be equipped with knowledge and strategies for successful navigation throughout your career, and your abilities to communicate, address challenges, and advocate for yourself effectively are crucial to successful navigation. Let's dive in to better understand the relevant lexicon.

Bias

The definition of bias can get complicated as there are many types and layers to bias. You can find an excellent description of various biases in an article titled "Types of Bias" on the CPD Online College knowledge base, written by psychologist Nicole Murphy.[22] Research suggests that there are hundreds of different types of bias. Murphy lists at least twenty types of bias—everything from the Dunning-Kruger effect (the inability to recognize your own incompetence) to affinity bias, which refers to the unconscious preference of people who are similar to you. There are a lot of ways bias creeps into our day-to-day lives!

As Murphy states, bias is an inclination, prejudice, preference, or tendency toward or against a person, group, thing, idea, or belief. Biases are usually unfair or prejudicial and are often based on stereotypes rather than knowledge or experience. Bias is generally learned, although some biases may be innate. Bias can develop at any time in an individual's life—so if you don't have one at the moment, don't get too comfortable; it can show up when you least expect it.

In some cases, the bias may be subconscious, and the individual may not be aware that they are expressing bias toward others. Although biases can sometimes be positive or helpful to the individual—such as experienced-based bias, whereby a business leader or engineer develops an intuitive sense for troubleshooting problems—in most cases, biases will be damaging.

Bias is usually based on stereotypes about an individual's physical characteristics or the group they identify with. Think of confirmation bias, where people favor information that aligns with their existing beliefs; racial bias, where assumptions are made based on someone's race; gender bias, where people are judged based on gender stereotypes; or ageism, where people are treated unfairly due to their age. These characteristics are often immutable, meaning they do not change over time. In the workplace, we typically see bias in the form of gender, age, race/color, and affinity—where you prefer people who look or behave similarly to you.[23]

Sexism

Sexism is prejudice or discrimination based on one's sex or gender identity. Sexism can affect anyone, but it primarily affects women and girls. It has been linked to gender roles and stereotypes and may include the belief that one sex or gender is intrinsically superior to another. Sexism can be explicit, like derogatory comments or slurs, or implicit, like unconscious bias in hiring practices or promotions.

Sexism manifests from individuals and institutional practices that limit opportunities, reinforce stereotypes, and justify unequal treatment based on gender.

At the individual level, sexism includes behaviors such as sexual harassment, unequal pay, and discriminatory hiring practices. In the case of Ellen Pao, Pao experienced sexual harassment, including one instance where a senior partner, Ajit Nazre, allegedly made unwanted advances and groped her during a work-related event. Institutionally, sexism appears through policies and unequal access to resources, opportunities, or representation, as illustrated in the Pinterest lawsuit brought by Ifeoma Ozoma and Aerica Shimizu Banks.

Common acts of sexism at the institutional level are typically systemic, meaning they're woven throughout the system, such as a disproportionate number of men in leadership roles and women in stereotypical nurturing roles such as HR or administration.[24]

Sexual Harassment

Employees are protected against sexual harassment under federal and state laws. Be sure to understand your state laws. Sexual harassment is a form of sexual discrimination under Title VII of the Civil Rights Act of 1964. This federal statute covers employers with a minimum of fifteen employees.

Many wrongly assume that the victim and perpetrator are always of the opposite sex, and typically female and male, respectively. However, as you will see in the story of Madeline in Chapter 4, a victim doesn't have to be the opposite sex of the perpetrator, and perpetrators can be of either sex or any gender identity.

Let's look at the types of sexual harassment: quid pro quo harassment, hostile work environment, and retaliation.

Quid Pro Quo Harassment

Quid pro quo is Latin for "This for that." Through the lens of sexual harassment, this is when a supervisor propositions a subordinate for sexual favors in exchange for a promotion, salary raise, or favorable shift assignment. Alternatively, quid pro quo harassment occurs when a rejection of a supervisor's sexual advances results in a tangible loss of job benefits. Once again, Ellen Pao's experience with Ajit

Nazre is a great example of this. Nazre, a partner at the firm, allegedly excluded Pao from important meetings and emails when she ended a sexual relationship with him.

Hostile Work Environment

I did not realize this was under the sexual harassment law until I did research years ago when I was being sexually harassed. Sexual harassment doesn't have to involve a direct request for sexual favors in exchange for favoritism or a promotion.[25]

A hostile work environment consists of conduct so severe or pervasive that it undermines a person's job performance or changes the terms and conditions of their employment. Examples include recurring episodes of unwelcome touching, lewd gestures, or sexual comments or jokes that make the work environment hostile. A severe incident, such as sexual assault, may create a hostile work environment by itself due to its severity.

The law doesn't prohibit simple teasing, offhand comments, or isolated incidents that are not very serious. However, harassment is illegal when it is so frequent or severe that it creates a hostile or offensive work environment.[26]

The harasser creating the hostile work environment does not need to be the victim's supervisor. They can be a supervisor in another department, or a coworker, customer, consultant, or executive. The harassment does not have to be accompanied by economic injury or an adverse employment action such as a demotion or loss of benefits.

The harasser's conduct must be unwelcome. If a victim banters with a harasser who makes sexual jokes, the employer can use this behavior as evidence that undercuts a sexual harassment claim. The victim should tell the harasser their conduct is unwelcome and ask them to stop. Also, the victim should use whatever grievance system is available through the employer before filing a complaint with the Equal Employment Opportunity Commission (EEOC), which enforces anti-discrimination laws.

Retaliation

Retaliation includes taking any adverse employment action against an employee who has asserted their right against discrimination. It is also unlawful for an employer to retaliate against a victim of sexual harassment for complaining to Human Resources, following grievance procedures, or filing a discrimination charge.

An employer also may not retaliate against someone who assists with an EEOC investigation. For example, a coworker of an alleged victim may be asked to testify in connection with a claim of sexual harassment. That coworker cannot be punished for providing truthful testimony, even if it corroborates the victim's claims against the employer.

Ageism

Ageism is the systemic prejudice, discrimination, or stereotyping of individuals based on their age. Ageism is typically thought of in the workplace against older workers, but as you will see in Chapter 5, it can also be against younger workers.

Like sexism, ageism operates at the individual and institutional level, influencing behaviors and policies that reinforce negative stereotypes about a person's capabilities, worth, and relevance based solely on their age. Common stereotypes for older workers include being technically inept and resistant to change. Harassment behaviors include condescendingly speaking to older workers or excluding them from discussions, projects, or activities.

Ageism is often institutionalized and appears in policies and practices such as mandatory retirement or biased hiring and promotional practices. Younger workers experience ageism when they and their ideas are dismissed as inexperienced or less capable due to their age and are excluded from decisions or leadership roles.[27]

Racism

Racism is prejudice, discrimination, or antagonism by an individual, community, or institution against a person or people based on their membership in a particular racial or ethnic group, typically a minority or marginalized group. Racism is the belief that different races possess distinct characteristics, abilities, or qualities to distinguish them as inferior or superior to one another. It involves a combination of racial prejudice and power, enabling one group to dominate and marginalize others. We saw that with Owen Diaz, the Black former Tesla employee who was racially harassed. He experienced frequent racial slurs and a hostile work environment.

At the individual level, racism includes overt actions such as racial slurs, hate crimes, and discriminatory behavior based on someone's race or ethnic background. It also involves more subtle acts of bias, such as microaggressions, discussed next.

Systemic racism includes policies and practices at the institutional level that cause disparity in hiring, promotions, and access that create and sustain racial inequities.[28]

Microaggressions

A microaggression is a statement, action, or incident delivered in an indirect, subtle, or unintentional way that causes discrimination against members of a marginalized group, such as a racial or ethnic minority. These can be as small as mispronouncing someone's name repeatedly or as big as making assumptions about someone's ability based on their race or gender.

The term "microaggression" was coined by Harvard University psychiatrist Chester M. Pierce in 1970, but it became more mainstream during the BLM movement. Chapter 7 is dedicated to this topic. An example: When someone compliments a person raised in the US on their English—"You are so articulate"—simply because they are not White.[29]

Moving Forward

There are many types of bias and discrimination in the workplace. It happens at any level of one's career and is persistent and pervasive. We have seen that employees who have spoken out have either won lawsuits or have forced consequences on corporations. Speaking up can drive change, and that change is desperately needed.

The ability to effectively maneuver within or around the situations and cultures you encounter is paramount to your success. You now have an understanding of the language and terminology that surrounds these situations. Communicating clearly and effectively is your key to success. In the following chapters, we explore each of these areas of bias, providing my and my colleagues' experiences as well as notable cases. I will share strategies and language for you to use in similar situations. We start with what I think is the most pervasive form of discrimination: sexism.

CLOSING THOUGHTS

This chapter explores high-profile cases like Ellen Pao's to shed light on the pervasive issues of workplace discrimination and defines the different types of discrimination to help you better recognize, understand, and address these challenges.

- **Discrimination can manifest in many forms.** This includes sexism, sexual harassment, ageism, racism, and microaggressions. Each of these has unique impacts on employees and work culture.

- **Systemic bias and exclusion can affect career advancement.** This is especially true for women and people of color.

- **We must fight bias.** Understanding discrimination and bias—and the emotional toll it takes on employees—is a positive step toward identifying, challenging, and removing these practices.

Sexism—The Cost of Being Female

"The test of whether or not you can hold a job should not be in the arrangement of your chromosomes."
—Bella Abzug, *Bella!: Ms. Abzug Goes to Washington*

GENDER BIAS STARTS EARLY in our lives with different expectations at home and in society. Social norms in many of our families dictate that girls are more fragile and need more protection than boys; boys mow the lawn, and girls clean the house. It shows up in our education systems; boys are smarter at math, and girls are better at English.

Although we have seen a shift in roles and responsibilities at home, with men increasingly taking on more childcare and support duties, the traditional gender roles, where men are the primary earners and women are the support system, persist in our collective consciousness. These biases and stereotypes show up at home, in our relationships, and at work.

Gender stereotypes—preconceived ideas of female and male characteristics and roles determined and limited by gender—are what fuel sexism in the workplace. It can take countless forms, from being interrupted in meetings to having our ideas dismissed until echoed by a man in the room to being passed over for leadership positions.

A Black woman once shared with me that when her company hired another Black woman, some colleagues commented, "Oh, now you have some competition." This bias isn't limited to race; many women have had similar experiences. The message wasn't just that women would only be rivals with each other (not with men), but that they had a limited opportunity in the company—as if there was only room for one. The message is clear: Women can only compete with each other, not with men. Sexism can be damaging to one's career, self-esteem, and mental health.[1] It can limit opportunities for advancement and promotion, thus affecting the ability to earn an adequate salary. It can lead genders into "default" work roles that represent the paths of least resistance—women taking jobs in HR and Marketing, men taking roles in Finance, Leadership, and Engineering, even if these people would excel in and prefer other roles.

Sexism isn't always obvious, blatant, or hostile. It can be quite subtle. It is so slight that we may miss it, or when we experience it, we may even doubt ourselves. I know I have.

I have seen and experienced much sexism throughout my career, but there were so many times when I doubted myself. Was that a sexist remark? Did he mean it that way? Am I being too sensitive? Was that a sexist remark or a racist one? As you move up in your career and there are fewer women in the room or, as was often my experience, you're the only woman in the room, the doubt runs deeper. When there are other women in the room and there is sexist behavior or a remark, it is easier to validate your feelings as you see the other women in the room tilting their heads to the side with a look of what appears to be confusion but is actually "Wow, he did not just say that, did he?" That collective "He sure did" validation is essential.

This chapter discusses various forms of sexism using examples from my experience, friends, and notable cases. We explore how to approach each, when to speak out, and what to say. We also weigh the importance of supporting others by speaking out for them or supporting them in the room when they speak out. Now, let's explore how sexism in the workplace might be showing up for you.

Women's Street Cred

Better known as the gender credibility gap, this refers to the phenomenon in which women are not perceived as being as credible as their male counterparts. Men are considered rational, objective, and intelligent, while women are emotional, subjective, and not as intelligent as men.[2]

Yes, this is a stereotype that is embedded in our perceptions of gender.

It isn't always conscious, but that doesn't make it less damaging. I'm sure you have seen it often. When a man speaks with authority in a meeting, we listen and assume what he says is true. He is immediately credible. But it's not the same for women. We have to earn our credibility. We often must over-explain to prove or make a point. Others in the room ask us more questions than they ask the men. Too often, men simply make a statement and everyone moves on.

The other way this shows up is when a woman offers an opinion and someone immediately asks one of the men in the room if they agree. I haven't seen this happen the other way around very often, if ever.

I was working in a company where there was another female executive. She was very good at her job. Anytime she was asked a question, she had the answer and the data to prove it. Even with that, if she stated an opinion or an action we should take, the CEO would ask the (male) CFO what he thought. Every. Single. Time. He didn't trust the female exec's opinion or value her expertise. Unfortunately, she never spoke to the CEO about this. If she had, how might she begin? Her approach could have been to set up a meeting or wait until her next one-on-one meeting, talk to him about it, and ask why he needed to confirm with someone else.

Here is how the conversation could go, even if it is your manager. "Hey, I've noticed in meetings that when I say something or offer an opinion, you ask X if he agrees with what I just said. Is there a reason you do that? Is there a reason you are not confident in my responses or experience?" He may say yes and give you a reason for it. Or he may say no and cover himself. You could then respond, "Okay, you may not realize this, but by doing that, you are undermining my credibility with my peers. I don't think that is good for anyone."

By speaking up and discussing the situation, you accomplish two things: (1) You might get insight into the information he feels you are not providing to give the whole picture—that is why he asks someone else, or (2) it may help raise awareness of his behavior and squelch it. He may slip up occasionally, but not without knowing what he just did.

Here's what happens if you don't discuss it with the person, whether that's your boss or a colleague. The more they ask someone else to confirm what you just said, the more they are devaluing you. If this continues, you risk not being promoted or, worst-case scenario, being let go. The woman I mentioned was let go. Perhaps her boss viewed her as weak and inexperienced in her role; perhaps if she had brought this behavior to his attention, he would have come to value her more, as would her coworkers.

"I'm Speaking"

Another way sexism can manifest is by being "spoken over" in a meeting—literally, while we are talking. Has this happened to you? I'm sure if we were in a room full of women and I asked this question, most of the room would raise their hands.

Vice President Kamala Harris brought attention to this idea when she held up her hand toward the person interrupting her and said, "I'm speaking." She didn't hesitate or say, "Excuse me, but I was speaking" or "Please, may I finish what I was saying?" She simply said, "I'm speaking," then continued. We saw her do this quite publicly in the vice presidential debate with Mike Pence in 2020. And we saw it again during her tenure as VP and when she ran for president.

I love it because she doesn't apologize or allow interruptions. She keeps on talking, not missing a beat. Too often we women tend to be apologetic even when it's the other people who are being rude and disrespectful.

Don't apologize. Women are taught at a young age to be aware of how their behavior affects others. Men are taught and encouraged to focus on themselves. It's not easy; it is a difficult habit to break. I even find myself saying, "May I finish?" or "Excuse me, may I please finish what I was saying?" But I am getting much better at it.

In one meeting, I wasn't just interrupted once; I kept getting interrupted by several men in the room. They took over the conversation. I had to say: "Guys, I *will* finish what I have been trying to say, and we will not leave this room until I do." It got a laugh—which is good—and they got my point. Humor is a great tool to use in certain instances.

When we encounter these situations, the if, when, and how of our response is essential to think through. It is not always easy when you are in the heat of the situation, but sometimes, it helps to take a breath, understand the intent, and decide how to respond.

Recently, I was presenting to another department. A male from the other department jumped in while I was presenting a slide and took it upon himself to explain my entire slide—I mean, my entire slide. I was furious, and in my mind, I wondered if he would have done that if I were a man presenting. I could have stopped him in his tracks and firmly said, "Thank you, Greg, but I've got this" or "Greg, I am speaking." But I didn't do that. Here is why: He was a young professional, had a new boss, and there had been discussions about whether the team he managed was even necessary. He might have seen this moment as an opportunity to showcase his expertise and value to his new boss.

So his intentions were probably not to speak over me because I was a woman—although I still don't think he would have done that if I were a man. If you had been in this same situation and addressed it with him, you would have been right to do so. I decided at that moment that it wasn't necessary. Of course, if he did it again, I would address it.

Stolen Ideas

In September 2022, Professor Nicole Gugliucci posted this on X: "My friends coined a word: hepeated. For when a woman suggests an idea and it's ignored, but then a guy says same thing and everyone loves it."[3]

Hepeating. I am sure you have experienced this in meetings. I have. Many times. I've offered an idea, there is a short silence or a shrug of uninterest, and then not even a few minutes later, a man says the same thing, and it gets discussed. The fact that a man was now saying it apparently gave it more weight.

I once had a boss and a peer that I swear were in cahoots when it came to this. Whenever I or another woman would offer an idea in a staff meeting, my boss would shrug his shoulders as if to say, "Eh, no thanks," and then my male peer would say, "Oh, we should . . . [insert what I or the woman just said]," and the discussion began anew. It happened so often we got tired of saying, "I just said that" or "She just said that." The men never apologized—never said, "Oh, sorry, didn't mean to steal your idea" or even "Sorry, I didn't hear that." They just shrugged it off as if to say, "Oh well."

This "hepeating" behavior is damaging because it takes away our value as women and gives it to someone else—a man. If someone in the room keeps getting credit for great ideas, guess which one will be promoted or viewed as a strong player in the organization?

So what should you do about this? If other women are in the room, you can support each other. Instead of saying, "Maria just said that," you can support by repeating what Maria said. "Great idea, Maria. That would help us solve Y." It is more difficult to dismiss the idea if it is repeated and a value statement of the concept is attached.

> To get other women to support you, start helping them. Lead by example—every time. They will catch on and return the favor.

To get other women to support you, start helping them. Lead by example—every time. They will catch on and return the favor.

According to *The Washington Post*, female staffers in Barack Obama's White House used a strategy called "amplification" to combat hepeating: "When a [female White House staffer] made a key point, other women would repeat it, giving credit to its author. This forced the men in the room to recognize the contribution—and denied them the chance to claim the idea as their own."[4]

If you are the only woman in the room, don't just state the idea; give it life. Tell a story around the concept. If you have examples or data that support the idea, then provide them. You may be brainstorming, but there is a reason you are presenting the idea, so state what the value of the idea is to the organization.

For example, you state that perhaps your team should create quarterly business meetings for your customers. You should not only state that idea but also say something like: "These meetings will allow us to check in with customers, ensure that our product is helping them meet their goal for the product, and allow us to offer suggestions for their transformational journey with the product. The customers will feel they are getting more value from our company and will be more apt to renew and upgrade."

The more you describe your idea or thought, the harder it is for the next person to take credit for it. Remember to remove tentative or weak language like "I just," "maybe," or "I was thinking," which can undermine your confidence and make it easier for others to dismiss or claim your contributions.

Remain Calm

Have you ever been told to "relax" when in a meeting? If the conversation gets heated and a woman is going toe-to-toe with a man, someone steps in to calm it down. "Okay, everyone, calm down. Let's move on." Sound familiar? As Taylor Swift once said, men can react, but women can only overreact.[5]

Apparently, seeing a woman giving it back to a man in a room makes many people uncomfortable. As we all know, being told to relax or "calm down" can have the opposite effect. It is provoking, patronizing, and a way for the other person to regain the control they lost.

How have I responded to this? I say something like this: "Oh, I am perfectly relaxed, and I think this point needs to be heard." They may still attempt to move on from the conversation: "Well, let's take this up when calmer heads prevail." Your response: "Again, I am calm (relaxed) but happy to discuss later if you need more time."

Here's the thing: Situations can arise anytime, in a meeting or throughout the day. Keeping a clear head at all times—even if provoked—allows you to detach yourself from the emotions you may be feeling and respond with authority and professional maturity. Responding this way wins every time, even if it doesn't feel like it in that moment.

Once you learn to respond calmly, people will notice your ability to handle difficult conversations well. It shows you have the qualities of a leader. Flying off the handle in a meeting doesn't work, especially for women and, most certainly, for women of color. You will be labeled emotional, angry, etc. Even if you are angry, you can find a way to say you're angry without actually showing anger.

If you have strong feelings about a topic in a meeting, you don't have to shout or show anger; you can say: "I am going to speak passionately for a moment about this." Say that, and then whatever you say next, make it crisp and concise and say it with authority. As I said earlier, using humor works too. It can lighten a room but allows you to get your point across.

Gender Roles

Yessi Bello Perez, in her article "Sick of Sexism in Tech?" writes: "I've personally lost count of the amount of times I've heard people (not just men) say the tech industry is completely open to women, but with the caveat that there are plenty of roles available in marketing, public relations, or human resources. [. . .] Can the industry only tolerate women when they perform jobs that are somehow viewed to be 'feminine'? As far as I know, identifying as female and being able to think or code aren't mutually exclusive!"[6]

As we covered in the chapter's intro, gender stereotypes limit many areas of our careers. Our job opportunity pool is severely limited if we seek only roles that align with traditional gender roles because we typically don't get hired for other roles. Being in these roles perpetuates the pay gaps, as these roles are normally paid less, so the economic inequity continues to widen. It leads to discrimination in hiring and promotion practices as male roles are often viewed as more important and showing leadership, while women, therefore, don't advance to higher levels at the same rate as men. It becomes a vicious cycle of perpetuating biased beliefs and the ensuing effects on women.

Then, there is the lack of job satisfaction. When we're not in the kind of challenging jobs we want, we end up feeling underappreciated. We are hindered from tapping in to our natural and valuable talents because we cannot enter certain professions where we may have more talent and success.

The Pay Gap

The gender pay gap—the difference between men's and women's earnings—has barely closed in the United States in the past two decades. In 2022, American women typically earned $0.82 for every

$1 earned by men, about the same as in 2002, when they earned $0.80 to the dollar.

The gap is worse for minority women, with Black women earning $0.70 to the dollar of a White man, nearly $1 million less than White men over a forty-year career. For all women, the gap increases as we age. Starting at 92 percent of men's earnings at age twenty-five, women's earnings fall to 83 percent by age thirty-five and drop further to 79 percent between ages fifty-five and sixty-four. This pattern has persisted for four decades.[7]

Being a parent also affects pay, but it differs for women and men. Among women with similar levels of education, there is little gap in earnings, whether a woman is a mother or not. However, fathers earn more than all other workers, including men without children at home, regardless of their educational level. This is what's called the fatherhood wage premium.[8]

I've seen this up close. Two people—a man and a woman—in my company held similar roles and worked in the same department. We were given the mandate to downsize. The female was a solid performer, and the male consistently failed to meet job expectations. When discussing both employees regarding a layoff, both leaders I was speaking to commented, "Well, he has a family to support." The female also had a family, and, in fact, she was the majority provider. When I brought this up, I got a shrug of the shoulders.

The idea that the man is the family provider and needs to make a larger salary or should be protected from layoffs is not uncommon. And it shows up in the gender pay gap. One of the leaders in this example was a woman; she shrugged her shoulders just as nonchalantly as the male leader did. It isn't just men who hold these biases.

The gender pay gap not only affects a woman throughout her career by earning, on average, 82 percent of what men make, but it also affects her in retirement. Since 401K contributions and company matching are based on a percentage of your earnings, lower wages mean lower retirement savings over time. This gap compounds, leaving women at a financial disadvantage long after they stop working. Our Social Security benefits are based on our lifetime earnings. As a result of women making less than men throughout their careers, women receive less Social Security and lower pension payouts. Women's retirement income is 70 percent that of men's.[9]

Some companies now have a pay transparency policy whereby everyone's salary is made public to all employees. This certainly helps, but not many companies do it. I, for one, have never worked at a company that did this.

What can you do to prevent the pay gap from happening to you?

Negotiate from a Position of Strength

Learn how to negotiate your salary from the start. Some states have salary history bans, which do not allow a hiring employer to ask about your previous salary. Because women are paid less, if their new salary is based on their old wage, the gender pay gap will continue. Find out if your state has enforced this law, which was established to prevent the continuation of the gender pay gap. Regardless of whether your state has a ban, HR and hiring managers may still ask this in an interview.

If I'm asked this question, I never answer it. Instead, I answer with the salary that I require. I have done my research and asked recruiters, so I know what someone at my level in my profession with my years of experience should make. Because I am an executive, I also get a bonus and equity in a company. This, too, can be tilted against women.

I rely on a friend to help with my research. A former colleague is a CFO and is kind enough to review my compensation offers before I accept a job. Find someone you have worked with in the past to review your offer for you; if you are new in your career, ask a friend or family member with experience in negotiating a salary to help you or check with a women's networking group.

When my husband and I moved to a new state, I went on a job interview. The company recruiter asked me what I'd been earning previously. Instead, I told him my salary, bonus, and equity requirements. He told me they were too high and that where we moved to was less expensive than my previous location, so my salary should be lower. I laughed. Then I said, "It doesn't matter where I am living; what matters is the value and experience you are getting from my years in tech marketing." I clarified that if they wanted my experience, they would have to adjust their offer. I was willing to decline the role if I didn't get what I asked for. In the end, I did get the compensation package I desired. But this victory was tempered by the knowledge that my husband never had to have this conversation with his company; they just paid what he expected, no questions asked.

I understand you may not be in a situation where you can walk away from a job; I have been there too. However, the employer doesn't know that. Don't give in so easily. Ask for what you are worth.

Keep these few things in mind when negotiating a salary.

- **Don't bring up salary too early.** Focus on discussing your experience and the value you can bring to the company. Your goal is for them to see you as the right candidate before diving into compensation.

- **Handle salary questions carefully.** Recruiters and hiring managers may ask for your salary requirements up front and often they will try to get you to state what your salary requirement is first. Instead of giving a number right away, highlight your interest in the role and your experience and ask for the salary budget for the position. If they insist on an answer before they show their hand, provide a range that works for you, ensuring your minimum is acceptable as they often start with the lowest offer possible.

- **Do your research.** Find out the typical salary for your role and industry by asking recruiters, people in your network or trade association, and colleagues in similar roles.

- **Consider bonuses.** If the salary is lower than expected, negotiate for a higher performance-based or sign-on bonus to fill the gap.

Here is a simple example of a salary conversation. Practice your response before an interview as salary negotiations don't always occur after the offer is presented.

HR: I have one last question for you. What are your salary expectations?

You: I would love to know the approved salary range for the role.

HR: Well, it depends on the candidate and their experience.

You: Understood. Well, my salary range is flexible, and I would prefer to learn more specifics about the role before we discuss that.

HR: Can you give me a range?

You: Sure, I am interviewing for similar roles, and the range is $120K to $140K. My flexibility on salary depends on the role responsibilities and other elements of the compensation package.

When you get an offer for the position, if you are not satisfied with the offer, you should negotiate it by reiterating your experience, your value, and what you know the market salary is for your years of experience. If they come back with a hard no, then negotiate for other things like a bigger bonus, equity (if they offer it for your level), or vacation time.

Your experience may be straightforward, but difficult exchanges are also possible. A prospective employer may "low ball" your initial offer to see if they can get the role filled for less than it's worth. They may also express an unwillingness to negotiate by repeating the same offer or explaining that the budgets are locked down. Negotiating with someone who doesn't appear eager or able to negotiate can be uncomfortable. They may employ good cop/bad cop ("we value your experience, but the CFO just won't budge").

Recognize these tactics and remain composed, focusing on your worth and the value you bring to the company. You need a clear understanding of what you actually need for salary, what you're willing to accept, and what would "make you walk away."

Coffee, Tea, or Note-Taking?

I wish I could see a display of hands from those of you reading this book about how often you have been asked to take notes in a meeting. It still happens. I've seen it. If you are the only woman in a room and are asked to take notes, or perhaps there are other women in the room, but you are the one they always ask to take meeting notes, how do you handle that situation? I would say, "I am sure everyone can take their own notes based on what is important to them. I want to pay attention and contribute to the meeting. I don't think I can do that if I am responsible for taking notes for everyone."

Now, there are situations where it makes sense, like if you take turns taking notes for a routine meeting or if someone is standing up speaking, not near their computer. If they say, "Hey, can someone write that down for me so I don't forget?" there is nothing wrong with that—that is teamwork.

I have noticed lately that when it is time to take notes in a meeting, if the person leading the meeting is a man, he will naturally look toward a woman, think better of it, and say, "Who can take notes?" Yes, workplace bias is becoming more generally recognized, but they still look toward women first—it is embedded behavior.

When I was coming up in my career, I would volunteer to take notes because I thought I was showing my dedication. I was incorrect. You are not showing dedication by doing that. You are devaluing yourself. Remember, it is feeding into a stereotype that has been around for years. If you are trying to advance your career, you want to contribute to the conversation rather than take notes so everyone else can contribute. Don't do it—don't sacrifice your value like that. Same for serving coffee.

Consider the Intent

All of this falls under "What is the intention?" If the intention of the ask is because they think you are less important or they believe that only women know how to pour a cup of coffee, then don't do it. If you are getting up to get a drink or a cup of coffee and want to ask if anyone else wants a cup of coffee, and this favor is often reciprocated, that is fine. That is being courteous to your teammates.

See the difference in intention? We shouldn't get so stuck or self-righteous that we forget to be polite. But if someone asks you to get coffee and you don't want to, you could say, "I'm in the middle of something right now; perhaps someone else could help you." Or jokingly say: "Oh, are you really asking a woman to get your coffee? I thought that went out ages ago." They'll quickly get the point.

If this makes you uncomfortable, go ahead and get the coffee, but be sure to discuss it with the person afterward, privately, or with your supervisor.

No Girls Allowed

Once, my boss was in town, and we didn't have time during the workday to discuss a topic that we needed to get to. He said we could go to dinner and talk about it then, but he was concerned about doing that because HR had told him that he should never go to dinner or get drinks with a female worker alone. I told him that was ridiculous (in this case), and I was happy to go to dinner with him.

The "boys only" mentality can prevent women from having equal access to their coworkers, bosses, and higher-ups. How often have you seen a group of men at work go out for drinks or go golfing together but never invite the women? I recently heard from someone that they found out their male colleagues were going to strip clubs together. We won't get invited to that, will we? She was stunned and deeply disgusted that this behavior still occurred, realizing that any man who enjoys entertainment that objectifies women is unlikely to view his female colleagues as equals.

Men are more comfortable around men. They don't have to be concerned about locker-room talk or using profanity; they can drink, play, carouse—without concern.

According to research from Miami University and the University of Cincinnati, women are 12 percent less likely to be represented in the C-suite when their CEO plays golf. Golf has a long history of being a male-exclusive space; many country clubs and courses originally banned women or limited their access. Women executives' compensation is also 13 percent lower than men's under a golf-loving CEO—compared to 8 percent lower when the CEO is not a golfer.[10]

This "good ol' boys' club" and the practice of meeting in single-gender environments prevent us from forming relationships with key business influencers. We lose opportunities to bond with our boss and chances to get performance feedback, important project assignments, and other such prospects. It also hinders our promotional chances.

It happened to another woman and me, and we spoke up to the CEO. "Hey, we'd like to go for drinks too. Why aren't we invited?" He was embarrassed, said he didn't realize we'd been left out, and then invited us. Yes, sometimes we must force our way in. The men may not be comfortable with it, but they never will be if they aren't put in the situation of having men and women together.

Learn to Play . . . Golf?

How do you combat this? How do you overcome the risk of not getting assigned to good projects or having access to insider information that can help you do better in your role?

Well, I did learn to play golf, and I can hold my own in a sports-focused conversation. But what do you do if you are uninterested or don't have time to keep up with sports or attend after-work events because of other commitments? You need to think about building relationships. I have had strong relationships with almost all of my male bosses.

When I find myself in a culture or situation where I am the only woman in a sea of men, and when I'm not invited to those events or bonding moments that cultivate relationships in the larger group setting, I focus on individual relationship-building. I take it one person at a time. Of course this isn't the same as spending time outside of work with your boss or peers and bonding socially. It is in these relaxed moments when we get to know each other on a deeper level. Shared experience plays a powerful role in building strong relationships. Still, I'm committed to investing time in relationship-building because I know how important it is to be successful for myself, my team, and the company.

I've learned to build rapport individually with key people, men and women. It is a matter of getting out of your comfort zone, and you may find it to be quite enjoyable as it allows you to get to know someone on a deeper level than you can in a group setting. Showing support to someone when they need it, being empathetic to a boss you know is under pressure, and being a trustworthy ally and teammate go a long way to building a solid relationship with your manager, coworkers, and others throughout the organization.

If there are women leaders in the company, take advantage of that, ask them to mentor you, and network at work and beyond work with influential women in your industry or area. Create a sphere of influence outside of the boys' club.

These are just a few of many examples of sexism that too many of us encounter daily as we go about living our lives. I hope these examples will make us all more aware of these acts and encourage us to respond in a way that makes perpetrators think.

Push Back and Don't Give Up

I have offered examples of how I have handled some of these instances during my career. Please take those examples and practice them. You may need to adjust the responses to match your situation, but I encourage you to build the habit of calling out these instances. It may initially feel uncomfortable, but it will get easier over time. Bringing awareness to a deeply embedded and pervasive issue requires getting comfortable with awkward situations. Having the support of other people in the room—men and women who share your disdain for these behaviors and are willing to bring awareness to them when they happen—helps change the behavior. Change can feel too slow, but keep at it.

You must speak out when you are subjected to a sexist act and support others when you witness it happening to them. It happens so often that it is easy to normalize, but we mustn't. Normalizing or ignoring it creates emotionally unhealthy work environments, devalues your contributions, and ultimately hinders your career and undermines your aspirations.

Remember that empathy plays a role in some of these situations, and thinking through someone else's intentions is important. Not all acts are intentionally sexist, and kindly being empathetic and bringing awareness to them can lead to meaningful change without turmoil.

Having said that, you will encounter situations where empathy is not warranted. We talk about these situations in the next chapter on sexual harassment.

CLOSING THOUGHTS

Sexism in the workplace often hides behind subtlety and outdated stereotypes, but its impact is real and pervasive. Recognizing moments of sexism, blatant or covert, is the first step toward dismantling ingrained biases and behaviors. By responding with clarity, professionalism, and support for others, we can build more equitable work cultures where everyone, regardless of gender, is valued and respected.

- **Gender stereotypes fuel workplace sexism.**

- **Sexism isn't always blatant.** It can be subtle like being talked over, having your ideas dismissed or facing biased assumptions.

- **Validation from others can be powerful.** It helps to reinforce that your feelings are valid and the issue is real. Build a supportive network internally and externally.

- **Respond thoughtfully and with authority, even in uncomfortable situations.** This helps maintain professionalism while effectively addressing the issue.

- **Support others and speak up when you witness sexism.** If we remain silent, we unintentionally normalize harmful behavior and hinder progress.

- **Practice some of the examples I've provided.** That way, you're ready when you encounter similar situations.

4

Sexual Harassment— That's Not a Compliment

> Please note that the content in this chapter can be triggering, as it includes experiences of sexual assault and abuse.

"According to your own findings, I was subjected to sexual harassment, assault and abuse . . . I will never be the same person. I have spent almost the entire last year fearing for my safety. There is absolutely . . . no reason why the investigation was so dysfunctional."
—Former employee of DeepMind, quoted in *Financial Times*

THIS STATEMENT WAS FROM AN EMAIL sent to DeepMind in August 2020. The former employee whom the *Financial Times* called Julia, to protect her identity, was speaking out about HR's mishandling of her grievance. She said it took them almost a year to resolve her case.[1]

In December 2019, Julia claimed that a senior researcher at the company had sexually assaulted her twice. He sent her a couple of documents, one in August 2019—a confessional document that included allusions to raping unconscious women and sexual addiction—and another document that contained "graphic and degrading sexual depictions of her."

It took seven months for Julia's case to be resolved, and the perpetrator was not let go until two months later. During those nine months, the company set no disciplinary action or restrictions for the alleged perpetrator. In fact, he received an award during that time, and he continued to contact Julia. However, Julia was told she couldn't speak to anyone in the company about the situation, not even her manager. The manager in the HR office told her to refrain from entering the building where the researcher worked, which was for her own safety. Since her manager was unaware of the details of the complaint, he nevertheless pushed her to attend meetings in that building.[2]

Can you imagine this situation—Julia having to go to work every day after being sexually assaulted by another employee? Companies' blatant disregard of many situations I address in this book is all too common. When employees bring grievances, especially ones as serious as sexual assault and harassment, to their Human Resource departments, they naturally understand the department must investigate both sides. Still, we assume we will be heard and HR will work to resolve the issue quickly.

Instead, what often happens is that HR focuses on the business or gets pressure from other, more influential people in the organization—people who want to protect the company. That protection may take the form of protecting the alleged perpetrator, who is viewed as more valuable to the organization than the person who brought the complaint. This happens all the time, especially since most complaints are brought by women against men, and these men are often valued and influential within the organization.

This chapter discusses many forms of sexual harassment, and approaches them through the experiences of myself, my colleagues, and other women. We look at solutions as we discuss the role of fear and doubt in these situations, and the decisions you must make. We then weigh each option, so you fully understand the ramifications of your decisions.

The experiences we discuss help to illustrate the devastation of sexual harassment in the workplace. This often happens in stages: shock, doubt, stress, uncertainty, and even job loss. First, there's the initial shock that it is happening to you; what did you do wrong? Then comes the ensuing doubt—Did THAT just happen? You're now faced with the stress of deciding whether to tell or to remain silent and still having to perform at work while the harassment continues. The emotional toll it takes as you navigate all of this and determine if you should stay or go, let alone the lasting effects long after you leave, can cause you to doubt yourself and fear finding a new job and working for someone else. What if it happens again?

All this because someone decided that you were a sexual object to be abused, not a human being trying to make a living!

There's privilege at work here. The violator felt confident enough to do those things because so many of them get away with it. Even if they get called out, their lives seldom change in the way the victim's does. It's downright demoralizing. But it's also something we must get out into the open and talk about.

My hope is that these shared experiences will help you feel supported, educate you on your options, and give voice to all of us who have experienced sexual harassment.

My Harasser

Julia's story resonated with me as I had a similar experience of sexual harassment and was deeply disappointed in how my company handled the situation. I felt unseen—utterly inconsequential to the company—to say the least. Here's what happened.

I was ecstatic when I learned our company was hiring a strategy consultant. As a young professional eager to learn and grow, I understood the value an outside perspective could have on my growth. He was lauded as an expert in branding and marketing strategy; we were all excited for him to impart his knowledge and expertise. The head of our division seemed especially happy to have this person on board and help propel our business forward.

The consultant was to meet with several of us individually to learn about the business and help shape the strategy. We initially met in the office, but eventually, he preferred to have our meetings over lunch. I quickly noticed that he made off-color and crass comments during these meetings. The comments always had an underlying sexual tone. Then he asked to meet me—alone—after work for drinks. I did not want to go. He made me feel uncomfortable. I tried to get out of it, but he kept pressuring me, saying it was the only time he could meet and we had important work to discuss. I didn't feel I could go to my boss; I intuitively knew that if I wanted to get ahead, I needed to be open to working after work hours. That was the company's culture—the "in crowd" often went out for drinks.

But his off-hand comments grew more suggestive and aggressive; he would make comments about sex and even sexual assault. For example, he often tried to bring in comments where he could use the word "rape." I could tell he was enjoying it—enjoying watching my discomfort.

As an aside, there are many details of this experience that I could go into here, but some experiences are simply too painful to recall. When we talk about the emotional toll these situations have on someone, we must acknowledge that this toll isn't only in that moment, but it stays with us—the victims—for years afterward. Just know that he was aggressive in his sexual harassment, and I was overwhelmed and exhausted from it.

I decided to go to HR. I wanted this to stop and didn't want to meet with this person anymore. I was uncomfortable in his presence and fearful of being alone with him. My HR representative listened to my grievance. She said I needed to tell him to stop. I was very uncomfortable with this suggestion, but she told me I had to do it as part of the grievance process.

So I did. I told him, but nothing changed. He kept doing it—the sexual suggestions and the triggering words. It went on for four to five weeks. And it was really getting to me.

I had several more meetings with HR. The HR rep was sympathetic and tried to help me. She then told me it was time to tell my boss, who was the division head. So I did. As I relayed the situation to him, I could tell that HR had already told him about the situation before I did. He was prepared.

He hammered me about the seriousness of the allegation I was making. He was angry. He repeatedly asked me: Did you tell him to stop? "Yes, I did tell him to stop," I said. But my boss didn't believe me. We met again to discuss the situation, and he told me he'd spoken with the consultant, who (of course) claimed none of what I'd said was true. The consultant even told my boss that I'd never asked him to stop. The blame was quickly falling on me—for bringing this up, for not being able to stop it, and for, yes, being accused of lying about it all.

In the end, my boss believed the outside consultant, not me, his own employee. Though to be fair, I was never quite sure if my boss believed him or if he took that stance merely because he thought the consultant was more valuable to him and his career than I was.

But when I went back to the HR rep, she shut me down. I can't remember her words exactly, but she said she couldn't help me because there wasn't enough evidence. There was no proof that this man used those awful words and images in front of me, which was obvious, because I was the only one there to hear them. It was his word against mine. I knew that my boss had gotten to her. The HR rep knew me; she'd been friends with my sister in high school. To her credit, she let me know—in so many words—that she disagreed with what she'd been told to do about me. I could tell she'd been pressured to stop helping me.

After that, my boss became hostile toward me. The rapport I had built with him was gone. In our one-on-one meetings, his hostility and disdain for me were palpable. Outside of the meetings, throughout the day, he ignored me. He no longer considered me part of the "in-crowd." I felt extremely alienated at that time. I wanted out of that company. I now saw the company as one that would protect men and not help women. I kept thinking, *I am the employee. This guy is a consultant. Wouldn't you think the company would defend me over a consultant?*

I felt stressed out, anxious, and disillusioned. Up until that point, I had certainly experienced and witnessed numerous acts of sexism and racism, but this was something entirely different. I did not feel safe or protected. I felt like I was replaceable, not in the sense of being replaced with another employee but more in the sense of canceling me out as a human being.

This situation deepened my understanding of how corporate America worked for men instead of women and how business was prioritized over the individual, even in the most egregious situations. What I expected, as I am sure many people who are sexually harassed do, was that my concern would be taken seriously, that it would be investigated immediately and addressed based on the investigation, and that I would be safe from retaliation.

Instead, I found quite the opposite. The company protected the man, even though he wasn't even an employee. They did not conduct an investigation, and I was not safe from retaliation but was actually punished for having spoken out.

I left the company not long after that, and I heard that after I left, several women came forward with complaints about this same consultant—and he was let go. The company must have reached a breaking point and knew they couldn't deny that man's behavior any longer. What frustrates me is that the company did not believe me alone; it wasn't until several women came forward that the company finally acted upon the allegations.

When Harassment Happens Outside Work

In Chapter 2, we examined how sexual harassment is a form of sexual discrimination under Title VII of the Civil Rights Act of 1964. We also noted that a victim doesn't have to be the opposite sex of the perpetrator, and perpetrators can be of either sex or any gender identity. We considered the three types of sexual harassment: quid pro quo, hostile work environment, and retaliation. In the case of Julia's and my stories, those would be considered hostile work environments. Mine also contained retaliation because my boss treated me differently after I reported my situation.

What you should also know is that sexual harassment doesn't need to happen at work. It can occur after hours and isn't always at work functions. A friend of mine—let's call her "Erica"—was at a sales kickoff event. At the final event of kickoff week, she and her teammates celebrated on the rooftop bar's dance floor.

Their boss, a vice president at the company—a long-time company man who was part of the "good ol' boys' club"—joined in on the dancing. At one point, he leaned in to congratulate a female coworker on a job well done. The VP grabbed her hand, twirled her to face him, and said, "My God, I'm dying to f—k you!"[3]

> At one point, he leaned in to congratulate a female coworker on a job well done. The VP grabbed her hand, twirled her to face him, and said, "My God, I'm dying to f—k you!"

Harassment doesn't have to be by a boss or another employee. It can be a customer or business partner—or an outside consultant, as was mine. The story I told in Chapter 1 was about a business partner trying to find out what hotel I was staying at and my room number while we were at a conference. On a separate occasion, he came to our office for a meeting, where he continued telling my (male) coworker, right in front of me, how beautiful he thought I was and how he wanted to take me on a date. I was already uncomfortable with what had happened at the conference when this man wanted my room number, and that day in the office made me feel even worse. I was stressed out, embarrassed, and angry that I had to tolerate such behavior. This was a partner creating a hostile environment for me. I told my coworker that I couldn't tolerate this anymore. He told his boss, who was the head of the division. He met with the partner and let him know that we would not be doing business with him.

Another time, an engineering consultant and I went for a drink after work. We talked about the product and work-related items. It was fine until we went to the parking lot to our cars, and he grabbed me and kissed me when we said goodbye. He wasn't an employee of the company, but the law sees customers, partners, and consultants as agents of a company, and therefore, this situation was—officially— sexual harassment.

But I didn't report it. I pushed him away and told him that it was inappropriate and that I was uninterested in his advances. I was young, maybe twenty-six, and didn't know his actions would be considered sexual harassment. Honestly, years back, women were so used to being "hit on" by men at work that unless it was a blatant act such as quid pro quo or a repeated act that created a hostile environment, most of us didn't even know it was something we could report. We just lived with it and moved on.

While there is still progress to be made in addressing the objectification of women, the advancements of women's movements in recent decades have led to greater awareness and a shift in societal norms. Today, these behaviors are less acceptable and, as a community, we have a clear understanding of what shouldn't be tolerated.

Abuse Comes in Many Forms

And as we said, it doesn't have to be someone of the opposite sex.

"Madeline" was in her office getting ready for a trip to Europe with her boss, who was the company's CEO. The CEO's assistant came into the office to give Madeline details about the trip. Madeline was distracted because she'd just gotten off the phone with her soon-to-be ex-husband. She apologized for being distracted and told the assistant the reason for her distraction—she and her husband were splitting up. That comment set off a storm of actions, leading to the assistant creating a hostile work environment for Madeline.

Unbeknownst to Madeline, the assistant was having an affair with the CEO. When the assistant realized that Madeline was soon to be divorced, she became concerned that the CEO would be attracted to Madeline, which could result in a separate affair, so she started blocking Madeline's access to the CEO. This resulted in hurting Madeline's ability to be successful in her job. The assistant had all the power; she had access to all the systems, the CEO's email, and his calendar.

Once, there was an essential meeting with a tech provider the company wanted to partner with. The tech provider wasn't happy. They insisted on flying in to meet with the executives of the company, and the CEO was to be in attendance. On the day of the meeting, the assistant told Madeline that the CEO wouldn't attend the meeting—it was believed she told him not to attend. Other executives were getting angry with Madeline. They insisted the CEO needed to be at this meeting—they were there to meet with him, the whole thing was an embarrassment, and they couldn't get the deal done if the CEO didn't attend.

But the assistant wouldn't budge. The CEO did not attend the meeting.

This behavior persisted for some time. Madeline even asked the CEO to talk to the assistant and make her stop, but he shrugged it off. He didn't want to upset the woman he was having an affair with.

According to Madeline, the other executives knew what was happening but didn't want to get involved because they feared losing their jobs if they confronted the CEO. The assistant persisted with different ways to keep Madeline from the CEO and degrade her in front of other executives. Finally, Madeline decided to hire a lawyer and file a lawsuit.

The company settled with Madeline to avoid public scrutiny, but the harassment didn't stop; it took the form of retaliation. After Madeline left the company, she started a consulting practice. She got a gig working for a new CEO, whom we will call Ben. Ben wanted to partner with Madeline's old company, as it would have been lucrative. When the CEO of her previous company found out that Madeline was consulting for Ben, he told his team that he would never become a partner if Ben didn't fire Madeline. Madeline and her lawyer sued them again.[4]

I share this story because when we think of sexual harassment, we assume it is a man harassing a woman. But sexual harassment comes in many forms, and I want you to be aware of them so that if anything like this happens to you, you will know that it is against the law and you can do something about it. For this to change, more of us must report it.

Reporting Harassment

Even though there is greater awareness of sexual harassment because of the #MeToo movement and more people in corporate America have been educated about it, not everyone will report it. Studies show that while one in every three women is sexually harassed at work, three-quarters of those women, a whopping three out of four women, will never report it.

If this happens to you—and I hope it never does—you will be faced with deciding whether or not to report it. I won't lie; there are cons, as I am about to discuss. But I will say this: Sexual harassment, depending on its nature, can lead to sexual assault, as we read from Julia's unfathomable experience at the AI company DeepMind. If you choose not to report it initially, but it continues and gets more aggressive, I encourage you to report it.

The reasons we don't report include worrying that we won't be believed, feeling embarrassed, and doubting ourselves—did I do anything to suggest it was okay? Was it my fault they did that?

Like the guy who grabbed me and kissed me after we had drinks after work. While I was driving home, I was angry for having put myself in that situation, for going and having a drink with a man—what was I thinking?! So I didn't tell anyone—not my boss, not HR—because I believed they would have thought I could have prevented it from happening in the first place. In a way, I was pinning the blame on myself before they could. I was protecting myself from having the situation become even worse.

We fear retaliation, and the numbers support that fear. According to the US Equal Employment Opportunity Commission, 75 percent of workplace harassment victims experience retaliation when they speak up.[5] Take the woman at the rooftop bar whose boss said to her, "My God, I'm dying to f—k you!" When Erica discussed it with her, the woman responded that she wouldn't say anything and didn't want my friend to either because it would be his word against theirs, and with a family to care for, there was simply too much to lose.

And look what happened to me when I reported my incident with the consultant: I was quietly sidelined by my boss. Before that incident, I was quickly moving through the ranks of my profession. But now I knew that would not happen anymore. I had to leave the company because otherwise, my career would have stalled.

The Consequences of Complaints

We may fear that people will find out, take sides, and have opinions. For example, when a VP slapped me on my backside as I was leaving his office, I told my boss. She laughed and told me she was sure he didn't mean it. She added, "He's a nice guy."

Some may not want to endure the turmoil of an investigation. If there are witnesses, they are typically interviewed as part of the investigation. You may not want to involve your coworkers. Perhaps you don't want them to know what happened. Very likely they may be angry with you for getting them involved. As a result, you may fear they won't accurately report what happened. Or they may decide not to participate, and you may feel animosity toward them. It can affect your relationships.

You may be hesitant to put yourself through the investigation. I can tell you firsthand that it is stressful, and while I was going through it—before I even knew the outcome—I felt *less-than*. I felt that the company wasn't doing enough, wasn't moving fast enough, wasn't supporting me enough, wasn't believing me to the degree that I needed them to believe me. Why weren't they just taking my word for it? Rationally, I knew they couldn't, but emotionally I needed them to.

The effects of these kinds of experiences are long-lasting. Even now, as I write this chapter, reflecting on my experience many years ago and asking others to relive theirs creates emotional stress for all of us.

If you are confronted with any form of sexual harassment, you will have to make a decision. Your options are the following.

- **Firmly, and I mean firmly, tell the person to stop.** As I have said, I have been in my career for thirty years. I am a CMO— chief marketing officer. I have seen a lot and experienced a lot.

Each of these instances make me more emboldened to speak out. Not as much in my early years, but times have changed, and women at all levels feel more empowered to speak up. If this happened to me now, I would have a conversation with the person, and in that conversation, I would tell the person I wanted them to stop. I would detail the incident(s)—when it happened and what they did or said. I would want them to know that I wasn't confused about the situation and knew it was wrong and potentially unlawful. I would tell them that I planned to report it to HR.

If you can, have this conversation while in the situation, but if not, because we are often too shocked to respond, have a conversation with them later that day or the next—as soon as possible.

- **Report it to HR.** Telling HR should get it on record in case the person tries to circumvent you by going to HR and telling a different story. So, for example, if you ask them to stop but don't go to HR, they could go and say you did something to them or that you accused them of something that didn't happen.

  Based on my experience with some HR teams, I would make it apparent that I wanted it documented. I would also write an email—and bcc it to my personal email (in case other people delete it or claim it was sent on a different date)—summarizing my meeting with HR: what I told them, what they said, any next steps, and that I asked them to document the situation. By the way, if you report it to HR, they legally have to investigate. But remember that HR is not there to be your friend. They are there to protect the company, not the employees. Relying on them to do the right thing for you can be wishful thinking.

- **Seek legal advice.** A lawyer can help determine if it is sexual harassment, whether you should report it, how to respond to the harasser, how to prevent the employer from retaliating after you report them, and what the exit options are. If your company doesn't resolve the issue or the harassment continues, I encourage you to seek outside counsel. You may think you can't afford a lawyer, but there may be instances when a lawyer will take your case, and you pay them once the suit is settled. Research or ask people you trust for recommendations for a good lawyer.

- **Leave your job.** You may decide not to say anything to the person or HR, or even if you do, you may decide that you don't want to work in that department or at the company. That is a perfectly acceptable choice. Making this decision isn't easy. You may feel angry and frustrated that you must leave a job and coworkers you enjoy working with. You may be concerned about a gap in your resume. The fear and turmoil of searching for a new job can be taxing. As we know, interviewing is stressful and an emotional rollercoaster in and of itself, let alone right after such a traumatic sexual harassment experience.

  However, you may not feel comfortable reporting it to your company, and even if you do, you may still want to leave and start fresh. If the person isn't called out for their behavior, they could repeat it with someone else, so perhaps you should mention it in your exit interview. We have to help each other by speaking up. Speaking up and creating awareness are powerful catalysts for change.

- **Do nothing.** This is an option for every choice we have in life. Do something or do nothing. There is no right or wrong answer here. It is what works best for you. However, if the harassment continues or elevates, I encourage you to consider the previous options. Your safety and mental health are what's important here.

  The decision to do nothing—not report it and continue working at the company—isn't an easy choice. You will still be reeling and experiencing mental stress from the experience, yet you must continue to perform at your job. You will be waiting for it to happen again; you may have lost trust in others and the company for hiring someone like this. Finding motivation to perform at your job will be difficult.

Questions to Consider When Deciding Your Course of Action

1. Will the person stop if I confront them?

2. Do I trust my HR department and company to do the right thing?

3. Do I need this job right now for financial reasons, or can I afford a gap in employment?

4. Do I have the money to hire a lawyer?

5. Can I continue to work in this company after this experience? If the perpetrator remains in the company and the company doesn't take appropriate action, what will my emotional state be like when I come to work every day?

6. How will I feel about myself if I don't report it?

7. Can I handle the emotional toll of reporting it? Am I ready to deal with the backlash and fallout?

I encourage you to think through your options, and no matter what you decide, please document everything from the first time it happens. You should send a detailed email to yourself. This creates a time-stamped message in the mail archive, which the company can't edit.

And get support from a trusted person—a friend, a therapist, a family member, etc. It is difficult to go through this; please don't do it alone. We can overanalyze the situation by casting doubt about our role in it and feeling unwarranted shame. It takes such an emotional toll and feels like a rollercoaster of many emotions—fear, anxiety, anger, doubt, and shame. This emotional toll can have lasting effects.

Take the case of one of my dear friends.

Kristine's Story

As soon as she turned on her video to join the call, "Kristine" heard, "I know I shouldn't say this, but you look fantastic." It was the CEO talking to her. She looked around the call and saw she was the only female present. The others on the call were all men from the senior leadership team. She was immediately taken aback and felt embarrassed. She didn't know how to respond, so she didn't.

This was two hours before Kristine would present to the board. It was her first time presenting to them, as she had only been in the company for two months as a VP reporting to one of the senior executives. She was still stunned by the CEO's comment as she presented to the board.

Months later, Kristine and several teammates were at dinner. The

CEO, sitting next to her, commented about not having to worry about dressing for dinner because he was a man. Then he said, "Kristine doesn't have to worry either, because she is always beautifully dressed." He didn't stop there. He started talking about his wife and then leaned over to Kristine, held her arm, and told her she looked like his wife. The way he looked at her as he said this left no doubt in Kristine's mind that it was a suggestive comment. He was flirting with Kristine.

Again, she was embarrassed as he said this in front of her coworkers and other executives. She didn't know what to say, especially in front of all these people, so she politely responded, "That's a nice compliment." But in reality, she didn't take this as a compliment— instead, she felt belittled, realizing she had accomplished so much, but here she was being made to feel like just a sexual object. After that, the evening was a blur. Kristine couldn't think straight; she couldn't converse. Her heart was beating so fast, her mind was reeling. She couldn't wait to get out of there.

The following day, a coworker who was at the dinner came to her and said that what the CEO had said to her the night before was sexual harassment, and if Kristine didn't report it to HR, she would. But when Kristine reported it to her boss, he stopped the conversation mid-sentence and said he needed to call the legal department and didn't want any more information. Kristine got the impression that he did not want to be involved.

A man from the legal department called Kristine a few hours later. He stated that the company took matters like this seriously. They arranged a time for Kristine to speak to their outside counsel and asked her to document what had transpired. An investigation began. She heard nothing for a few weeks. In the meantime, she had to work with the CEO daily because her role required it.

Eventually, Kristine was told that her story had been corroborated, that the board—an all-male board, by the way—had been notified, and that it had taken appropriate action.

She had no idea what the "appropriate action" was. The flirting man was still in the corner office as CEO. She didn't know whether she was a sitting duck or would be left alone. She was concerned because she had brought other women into the company. Because she had reported the incident, she had to assume she was shielded from being fired and stayed.

Little by little, she saw the CEO harassing the other female VPs about their work and then letting them go. They had started with eight female VPs and went down to two, including Kristine. The company moved Kristine to a new role. Things were okay for about seven months, and then she started to notice that when she proposed new strategies for her team, things stalled. She couldn't get anything done. They took away part of her team and her budget. Her new boss didn't understand why this was happening; he was also frustrated. Then it happened. Kristine was no longer protected.

Her boss called her and said that the company had to make some tough decisions. He gave her two options: (1) leave the company now, or (2) fire one of her employees and take that job, but at two levels below her current level.

HR then told her they had hired a new VP. Essentially, they replaced Kristine with a man, giving him only half her responsibility but with a full VP title.

So Kristine called a lawyer. Her lawyer told her not to commit to or sign anything. They tried to negotiate a severance package. The company didn't want to give Kristine a reasonable package; they wanted a non-disclosure so Kristine couldn't talk about the situation or the company to anyone. Kristine and her lawyer had to threaten them with staying and taking the lesser job that didn't require a gag order. The company eventually agreed to the package.[6]

Emotional Toll Lingers

I bring this story to you because of how it affected Kristine. Kristine was at the peak of her career. She was—is—great at her job. I can attest to this because we worked together. She is intelligent and motivated and has mastered her profession through hard work and a discipline to innovate. Now, she was out of work—for the first time in her career. Her career was stalled not because she wasn't performing at her job but because a CEO decided he liked her looks and wanted to flirt with her and because she dared to report the sexual harassment.

I know Kristine well. She gets up early in the morning, jumps on her Peloton, and gets ready for her day. She pours everything she has into her workday. She is relentless. She is a force. Or she was until this happened.

Then I saw her change. She couldn't get out of bed, lost energy, and doubted herself. She was unsure of the future. She was out of work for nine months, going from busy to not knowing how to fill her day. It was horrible to watch. She was getting depressed. I could hear it in her voice when we talked on the phone. In one conversation, she said, "I just mow the lawn. I mowed until I couldn't mow anymore." I knew then that Kristine was losing something vital to her—her worth.

Eventually, Kristine secured a new job offer. She was excited about the opportunity. However, because of her recent experience, she asked about their DEI and sexual harassment policy and wanted to see the company handbook. The hiring manager told her that the company didn't have a handbook. They were an HR-free zone, meaning they had no HR issues. He then told her that because she had asked for these documents, the company decided she was a legal liability and rescinded their offer.

Kristine was shocked. She had simply asked if they had policies to protect employees—and her candidacy was rejected just for asking. She spiraled. Her depression worsened. She couldn't figure out how to manage her days. She felt like she had no value. She was unsure if she could ever get her career back. She thought that somebody had stolen all she had accomplished.

What Kristine experienced is not uncommon. The potential destruction of a career, or at least a stalled career, along with the emotional turmoil we experience because someone else decides to be a predator happens more often than we realize, because we usually suffer in silence.

Thankfully, Kristine persisted. As of this writing, she is in a job she loves and is thriving again. Kristine took her experience as she applied for new roles and defined her boundaries. She knew what she would and would not tolerate at a company. As she sought employment, she continued to question their DEI practices. She reviewed their male-to-female ratio. She asked many questions about the culture, how career opportunities and promotions were determined, and how success in her role was measured.[7]

Kristine's experience offers two important lessons. First, we can experience horrible situations at work. It's crucial to stay vigilant and work to prevent them from happening again—to ourselves and others. Second, we must take our experiences, learn from them, and define what is acceptable for us. There are good companies out there. Define what reasonable means to you—what culture you want to be a part of and what you will and will not tolerate.

It Wasn't Your Fault

Sexual harassment can come in many forms; it can range from verbal transgressions to sexual abuse or assault. It can be unwanted touching or offensive comments or gestures. It can be verbal, visual, or physical. It doesn't have to be asking for a sexual favor in exchange for a promotion, a raise in salary, or getting the best assignments. It can be someone creating an atmosphere that makes you uncomfortable to work in—a hostile environment. It doesn't have to be a man against a woman. It can be any gender identity against anyone. It can be covert and subtle, but that doesn't mean it's okay.

When it happens, it can shake you to your core. It affects your ability to work, feel safe, and trust. Like many other types of discrimination in this book, it can disillusion you about the tech industry, the corporate world, or your career. It can affect how you "show up" in your next job or company and how you form relationships at work. When trust is broken, it can permeate through many other areas of our lives, as we saw with Kristine.

Talking about my experience with others—professionals and friends—helped me. As much as we shouldn't need it, I did need validation that what happened was wrong. Seek that support. Talking to someone as soon as you experience a situation that is blatant or simply feels off will help you validate the situation faster and do something about it immediately. Do your best to deal with your feelings to gain perspective on the experience and not let it negatively affect you. You did nothing wrong; you didn't deserve what happened to you. It wasn't your fault.

As we have seen with the #MeToo movement, speaking up can effect change. More women feel empowered to speak up because they see other women do it, which puts perpetrators on notice. I believe that more women and men who witness such behaviors will also speak up to support the harassed person—not everyone, but more than in the past.

Discrimination takes many forms. It isn't always gender-related, like sexism, or sexual, like sexual harassment. Discrimination can happen when people and corporations feel you are not worthy of being in your profession because of your age. In the next chapter, we discuss ageism, who it affects the most, and how it presents itself.

CLOSING THOUGHTS

Sexual harassment is a personal and often traumatic experience that can leave lasting emotional scars. It can occur in many forms—verbal, physical, or visual—and may happen in or outside the workplace, by people of any gender or position. The decision to report harassment, address it yourself, or not address it at all is a complex one, and it's essential to seek support, document everything, and carefully consider your options before taking action. Protecting your emotional and mental well-being should always be a priority, and no one should ever face harassment in silence.

- **Sexual harassment can happen anywhere.** This means at work, at after-hours events, or even outside of professional settings. It can be perpetrated by anyone, not just a boss or colleague.

- **The emotional toll of harassment is real.** The decision to stay or leave a job can be stressful and the long-term effects may linger long after the harassment occurs.

- **Document everything.** Send a detailed email to yourself. This creates a time-stamped message in the mail archive, which the company can't edit.

- **Know your options.** Whether it is confronting the harasser, reporting to HR, seeking legal advice, or leaving your job, understand the potential consequences of each decision.

- **Seek support.** Don't go through this alone. Reach out to friends, family, or a therapist for emotional support and guidance throughout the process.

Ageism—The Expense of Experience

"I'm stunned! Just had a recruiter inform me that I'm supposedly
too old for a software developer role. He had the audacity
to say, 'Your age makes people question why you haven't
moved up to CTO or something. I can't pitch you to clients . . .
Guess it's time to consider dyeing the hair, huh?'"

—Vern Six, LinkedIn Post, 2024

YOU MAY WONDER why we are discussing ageism, as you may be far away from that career stage. You may be in the building phase and concerned with the here and now, but it's important to understand what is coming. Ageism happens in the tech industry earlier than in most industries, as the median age in the tech industry is thirty-one compared to forty-two in the US workforce.[1]

The critical message for you to take away from this chapter is how you can maintain a long career. How do you stay on the course that you are building now? Building a career is a lot of hard work. It involves long hours, having to prove yourself, going the extra mile, getting in front of and building relationships with the right people. It means dealing with all of the topics in this book.

You don't want all of your efforts stripped away because you are no longer "the right age." You may soon realize that you are never the right age. You are either considered too young to be taken seriously or too old to understand technology and keep up with innovation.

We examine these biases in this chapter, and I help you learn about the varied types of ageism. I share my experiences with ageism and the experiences of others so you can identify when it is happening to you, as ageism can be very subtle. Lastly, I share strategies for maintaining a long career.

I recommend you start practicing these strategies now. I started early and maintained my discipline, and you may need to as well. You could still face ageism, but by staying vigilant, you can reduce the negative consequences of aging within the tech industry—and beyond. It's far better that you are the one to decide when you want to conclude your career journey, rather than letting some corporation or recruiter decide for you, as we saw with Vern's experience in this chapter's epigraph.

Normalizing Ageism

Vern Six's post went viral, with over two million impressions, thousands of reactions, and hundreds of reposts. It shows how many people experience ageism in the workplace. In the tech industry, anyone over thirty-five is considered old. They are viewed as having more difficulty processing information and picking up new things. They are also regarded as unable to keep up with the latest technology, while their younger coworkers are considered digital natives.

As noted earlier, the median age in the US workforce is forty-two; in the tech industry, it is thirty-one. According to Payscale, the median age at Facebook is twenty-eight, thirty at Google, twenty-nine at LinkedIn and Salesforce, thirty-three at Microsoft, and thirty-six at IBM.[2] According to Mark Zuckerberg, in a 2007 statement to a Stanford audience, "Young people are just smarter."[3]

We are surrounded by ageism in the US. We do not respect or honor older employees, and we frequently perpetuate ageist stereotypes. Take the blatant ageist ads that LinkedIn posted in November 2023. One ad portrayed a gray-haired woman sitting in her living room, looking confused as she talked about her son selling clouds. Another ad features an older man sitting at the dining room table, expressing his concern that he no longer understands his daughter. "I don't know how this happened. She was speaking in complete sentences before she was 2, and now she just mumbles all these alphabets"—he meant things like LOL, IRL, etc.—"I blame myself. I should have been around more," he choked out with emotion.[4]

How did LinkedIn, the largest business networking site in the world, approve these ads without even a clue that they were ageist and might provoke severe backlash? Because we normalize ageism. Everywhere.

There is an abundance of ads for antiaging potions and surgeries. We celebrate when we hit significant birthday milestones with cards that make light of our memory, wrinkles, and gray hair. TV commercials for older people are primarily about their ailments. Once I joined the over-fifty crowd, I noticed this happening more. This will happen to all of us. I experience it at work, doctor's appointments, and grocery shopping. I am treated differently—dismissed, spoken down to like I am a child because I am "older." I am just waiting for people to start shouting when talking to me to be sure I can hear them!

Those in charge of creating and approving these ads didn't think anything of it. They didn't consider it to be wrong. They thought it was funny and true. They knew that many also believe that older people can't understand, keep up with, and are confused by new technology.

Ageism reveals itself in many situations; it can be how someone refers to your experience, how you are treated in interviews, your inability to get interviews, or how you are treated at work compared to less experienced and younger workers. It can be bold and systemic, as in the case of IBM, which I explore later in this chapter.

My Brush with Ageism

One beautiful summer day in Boston, I felt ageism acutely as I walked to an interview. I enjoyed the walk and thought this would be a great section of town to work in. I arrived at the front entrance, which was all glass, and peered inside as I grabbed the door handle to open the door. And then I saw someone fly by on a skateboard. When I entered the building, it was colorfully decorated, had a foosball game table, and had all of the modern amenities that were designed to attract younger workers—folks in their late twenties and early thirties. I was forty-seven years old at the time. My first thought was that I would never get this job.

I pulled myself together as I was scheduled to meet with the CEO and a few others. The CEO was bright, and he was young. We had a long conversation; he asked my opinion, which was a good sign. As a follow-up, I was asked to "do a project"—which I did. I spent about eight hours on it. I was thorough because I wanted the job. It was an up-and-coming industry.

I was called back for interviews several times, meeting with a few more people each time. I met with the CEO to go over the project I had done. I got the sense that he was asking me questions not to understand if I was a good fit for the role, but because he wanted to learn about how other companies operated, as he was a new CEO and founder. I felt this when I met with the cofounder of the product team. He asked many questions, pumping me for information about how other companies' product marketing and product management worked. I had the same sense when I met with others—over eleven interviews.

But I never got a callback.

You may read this and think this wasn't ageism; I was simply going through an interview process. Maybe. But I trust my instincts. It was the questions they asked. They asked questions about how a process or department was run—like the product team or customer service teams. These were not questions about the marketing strategies I employed in the past or about my performance. They were trying to learn about the industry through my years of wisdom. And, yes, that happens in interviews, people try to get as much information out of you as possible.

However, it was that and everything else about the interviews. The culture—I did not see anyone over their mid-thirties. Each person seemed uncomfortable talking to me. Part of the interview process was having lunch with a few folks. It was so awkward. They just didn't know what to talk to me about because I wasn't their age. In conversations, they tried hard not to say I was old, stumbling over their words and saying I was experienced. It was how they said it and how they approached our conversations. They were interested in learning and yet were dismissive at the same time.

Sure, you could say this was *my* hang-up with my age, not theirs. Yes, I was uncomfortable, but that's the point, right? I was uncomfortable because there wasn't a single person there I could relate to. It wasn't an age-diverse company.

While interviewing, I have had similar situations over the years, and I could quickly tell they thought I was too old for their company for the same reasons and feelings I noted from this Boston interview. I wasn't sure if they didn't think I was a good cultural fit, if they assumed I wouldn't be up to date with tech, or both. It is frustrating to finally have the experience you've worked many years to get, only to be unwanted by a company because of your age. With a median age of thirty-one, the potential for ageism in tech occurs earlier.

The other way that ageism has shown up for me is in how I am treated or addressed. When talking to me, one CEO often said, "Well, you are very experienced." What he meant was—you are old. I know this because of how he said it. It was the hesitation when he said it. He knew he needed to be careful and not say "old." That's the difficulty with ageism. It's often hard to combat as it can be so subtle. I know the difference, as other CEOs positively mention my experience.

Another CEO, new to the company, would say in staff meetings, "We need more young people in this company." I had to laugh as I looked around the room—it was a group of gray-haired White men and me—yes, I have gray hair too, but I dye mine. Most of the men lowered their eyes with tight but neutral expressions. No one challenged him. We had all heard this before.

It wasn't simply a call for fresh talent; it was a message: *You are too old. You are not what this company needs to succeed.* It was not explicitly said, but the implication was impossible to miss. In reality, the problem wasn't a lack of youth in the company, as there were plenty of young employees; it was his unrealistic expectations, his need to shake things up, and his leadership style that seemed to thrive on making people feel inadequate.

For these seasoned professionals in the room, who had spent years building the company, it was more than an insult. It was a warning. To the CEO, their experience was a liability, not an asset. But, as is often the case, no one said anything. We just moved on.

Women—Potential Sexual Partners or Irrelevant Relics

That is the thing about aging in this industry—we older, more experienced workers are often not seen as valuable. This industry prefers to have a mostly young work population. Not to mention the double standard between men and women. Men are seen as growing older and wiser, while women grow older and lose value. Early in our careers, we are potential sexual partners (think: sexual harassment); later in our careers, we are irrelevant. We women are either being hit on or discriminated against, based on our age.

> We women are either being hit on or discriminated against, based on our age. So we find ourselves desperately trying to hold on to our jobs, and if that means going to the hairdresser every couple of weeks to wash away the grays, then we do it.

So we find ourselves desperately trying to hold on to our jobs, and if that means going to the hairdresser every couple of weeks to wash away the grays, then we do it. We are forced to try to look younger than we are. It becomes a big source of stress while we still work, trying to quell the fears of being let go and never finding another job. We can often tolerate behaviors that we shouldn't, simply in an effort to stay employed.

Some people condense the years of experience on their resume. I find myself stumbling over my words when introducing myself and saying how many years of experience I have. Should I say over twenty? Or twenty-five? Or over thirty? Which will be acceptable in this situation? Which response will not cause the other people in the room to gasp loudly or, even worse—take note of it for another time, like the next time there are layoffs? I think about this a lot, and I am sure I am not alone.

It's a ticking time bomb.

I am waiting for the day that I will no longer be hirable. I have seen it happen to many of my colleagues. They reach a certain age (somewhere over fifty), get laid off because their company was acquired or merged (not uncommon in high tech), and can't get another job. They are "forced" to retire.

Ageism is real, and it can be difficult to prove unless a company discriminates against multiple people, as was the case with IBM.

IBM's "Dinobabies" Case

In August 2022, IBM settled an age discrimination lawsuit brought by Denise Lohann, wife of a former employee who she claimed killed himself after being laid off by the company. He was fifty-seven at the time and had been with IBM for fifteen years. Documents that were unsealed as part of the case detailed the communications of two IBM executives regarding older IBM employees. The documents showed that one executive applauded the use of the term "dinobabies" to describe older IBM workers as part of a plan to remove them from IBM's workforce and explained his plan to "accelerate change by inviting the dinobabies (new species) to leave" and make them an "extinct species."[5]

In October 2023, IBM faced another age discrimination lawsuit brought by two HR leaders, Pamela Wimbish and Patricia Onken. Wimbish and Onken, both in their sixties, were long-time employees with high performance records, but were terminated, while much younger and less experienced people filled their roles.[6]

In March 2024, IBM faced additional age discrimination lawsuits. Sixteen former employees filed suit against them, claiming they were laid off to be replaced by younger workers. IBM has a history of age discrimination allegations.[7] In 2018, a ProPublica investigation revealed its discriminatory practices in replacing older workers with younger ones.[8]

Age discrimination can be difficult to prove unless it is systemic, like IBM's, but a law protects employees against ageism. The Age Discrimination in Employment Act (ADEA) of 1967 protects employees and applicants who are forty or older from age-based discrimination in hiring, compensation, promotion, discharge, terms and conditions, or privileges of employment.[9]

You should know that, as of the writing of this chapter, from a federal level, it is still legal for an employer to ask you your age, your date of birth, or your graduation date. At a state level, California, Connecticut, Minnesota, Pennsylvania, and Wisconsin prohibit questions about age during the hiring process.[10]

Like sexual harassment, there are several types of age discrimination you should be aware of.[11] Even if age discrimination seems like a distant problem, it does impact younger workers. In that case, it's often the reverse—being too young to be taken seriously or given responsibilities. At all ages, then, we find that too often, an individual's ideas and experiences are not properly valued.

Here are some of the subtle ways ageism can curb your career prospects.

Harassment

When derogatory or offensive remarks about your age are so intense and severe that they create a hostile work environment or prompt an adverse employment decision, you can't do your job properly. This can include such drastic outcomes as being demoted or fired. Examples of ageist statements include: "This might be too technical for you to grasp," "Perhaps this job is getting to be too much for you to handle [at your age]," or "Your views or experience on this are outdated—that's not how things are done now."

Discipline

You experience unexplained disciplinary actions at work, such as being written up or verbally called out for something your younger peers do but they don't receive disciplinary action for. Examples are being late for a meeting or not attending a social event. These discrepancies in how you are treated can leave you feeling singled out and questioning the fairness of workplace policies and expectations.

Direct Evidence

If you are told you are too old for something—it can be verbal or written—such as your boss saying that you are being fired to allow room for fresh experience or someone with more energy, that is ageism. If you are in a performance review and your boss says, "It might be time for you to step aside and allow the younger generation to have a try at this," that's overt ageism. Pay attention to your conversations with your boss during performance reviews and one-on-one meetings. They may approach it underhandedly by asking you what your five-year plan is.

Hiring and Promotions

Age should not influence hiring or promotions decisions. It should not be a determinant factor from the interview to the selection process. This also holds true during the promotion process. It can be challenging to prove; however, if you find an interviewer referencing your age, such as saying you are too experienced and they prefer someone younger, that could be age discrimination. If an employer hires someone younger and you know you have more experience, the employer would be responsible for proving they hired that person for another legitimate reason.

The same examples apply to promotions. If you are performing well in your role but are passed up for a promotion and a younger worker who is less qualified is promoted, you have the right to question that promotion. If you sense foul play in a hiring process or a promotion, document everything that is said or occurs as it is happening.

Some hiring companies have gotten smarter about this. They review resumes and can determine your age based on your years of work experience or if you put the dates of education—which I recommend you leave out. They simply won't call you for an interview. Some job postings say they seek people fresh from college or grad school. This is one tactic to get around age discrimination. They also know how to word things carefully, so pay attention to what they are truly saying to you.

I recently read a LinkedIn post about a guy who couldn't get an interview. He tried for months to no avail, so as an experiment, since he wasn't sure if it was his qualifications or his age, he removed a number of jobs from his LinkedIn profile. He immediately started getting solicitations for new jobs.

Exclusion

Exclusion is when your company subtly tries to push you out due to your age. You are no longer invited to training on new technology or processes, strategic meetings you once participated in, conferences and events, or even company events. It may appear as, "Oh, you don't need to go to the conference; we have Jim going, and he will have a lot more energy. You probably don't want to go anyway." It may start small but then become a pattern of exclusion. Again, document every occurrence.

Proving Your Case

If you get to the stage where you feel you need to take legal action, you're going to need proof. For an age discrimination case, you would have to prove some of the following:

- You are in a protected class—at least forty years of age.

- You were replaced by someone younger than you.

- When being replaced, you were performing your job responsibilities.

- Younger employees with similar capabilities were treated better.

- A policy was implemented that detrimentally impacted and targeted older workers.

- You consistently experience ageist comments at work.[12]

As I often do, you may be feeling that there isn't anything you can do about the discrimination of ageism. It happens a lot in tech, and yes, it will happen to you. This is a frightening proposition for many of us. I want to be the one who decides when I retire; I don't want it forced upon me. You may also believe you are not ready to retire because you still have much to offer. Despite what employers think about people over fifty, you know you still have the energy and desire to contribute to this industry.

I finally know my job very well, meaning that I have now experienced all aspects of the marketing profession for B2B SaaS. Through the lens of marketing and as an executive, I have worked through many situations that arise in business—startups, stage-ups, and turnarounds—and now, I can apply that knowledge with the greatest of skills. And I can impart that knowledge to others.

Focus on These Actions

No matter what age you are now, there are things you can do to avoid being pushed out or at least delay it. Don't wait until you are at the career stage where you are concerned about aging out. Employ these strategies now to combat ageism for as long as you can.

Stay Relevant

One of the reasons tech companies want younger workers is because they believe in the stereotype that older workers can't keep up with technology and are no longer relevant. Well, we know that isn't true. We created the foundation of technology that exists today. Of course we understand technology. However, I have seen experienced people stagnate in their profession. They do not try to keep up with the professional advances or technology. Each profession in tech, be it product management, customer success, IT, or marketing, evolves, and you must evolve with it.

I will use my profession as an example. Marketing has evolved over the years because of market dynamics and technological innovations. We went from direct mail and telemarketing to websites and online advertising (Google Ads) to email marketing, social media, marketing automation, search engine optimization, content marketing, account-based marketing (ABM), omni channel marketing, customer experience (CX), and now augmented reality (AR) for product demonstrations and advanced AI for greater predictive analysis.

The emphasis has switched from brand marketing to demand gen and revenue marketing to a combination of brand and revenue marketing, all supported by the evolutions just mentioned. As you can see, this is a lot to keep up with. I know many marketing professionals who gave up during the phase of marketing automation and revenue marketing (around 2010). I had many peers who said, "I'm not doing that. I am not learning that." Fear, stubbornness, laziness—whatever the drivers—left them irrelevant.

I have dedicated myself to my profession and I continue to master it. I attend conferences and webinars, read articles, and network with others with experience in these areas. I learn everything I can and then apply that knowledge at work. Do I fail sometimes? Of course. Failure is part of the learning process.

Staying relevant in your profession is the most impactful thing you can do for yourself. I love my profession, and I love learning, so this comes easy for me. If you don't, consider this: Your ability to demonstrate that you are keeping up with technology and new methods in your profession can significantly counter the stereotypes of the older worker who cannot grasp innovations and is less adaptable. Remember, your goal is to remain employed until *you* decide you want to retire.

Network!

Networking allows you to build a robust ecosystem of people you can reach out to when you need help or want to brainstorm ideas. These people can be your support system when you face a troubling situation and need another perspective. These are people you can learn from; they may have experience in an area of your profession that you don't, and they may have used a new technology that you can benefit from in your job. Often, they can also be the source of new job opportunities.

The term "networking" gets a bad rap. It isn't that difficult. Stay in touch when you meet someone—at work or an event—who you find interesting or who is knowledgeable about an area of your profession where you are not. Meet for coffee—virtual or live—and simply have a conversation. Do this regularly. I typically meet with someone in my network at least once a week. It could be various people from previous jobs, consultants I have worked with, or people I have met at conferences. I mentor people; people mentor me. Again, it's not that hard.

Don't underestimate the power of a strong network.

Promote Inclusivity

If you hear ageist remarks at work, whether directed at you or someone else, speak up about it. Don't let them pass. Say it kindly and with respect but say it. Pointing it out when it happens makes people aware that it is wrong and they will be called out for it when they do it.

If you work in a culture that has normalized age discrimination, encourage your HR department to include ageism as part of any bias training.

If you are younger and reading this, that means you too—don't be a part of the discrimination; be the change agent for it. You, too, will age. Work toward removing ageist practices from the workplace; your future self will thank you.

The law protects people over forty against ageism, but there is a practice of ageism against younger workers as well. I remember being in my late twenties and realizing that management or more senior workers didn't take me seriously. My ideas weren't always considered the same way as those of other workers. I often heard things like, "Oh, you are young; you don't get this now because you haven't been around long enough," or "I've been doing this for a lot longer than you; trust me, I know this better than you." Just because I was young and didn't have the same amount of experience, it didn't mean that I couldn't grasp the concepts and offer helpful ideas.

In these situations, I used to think, "I can't wait until I am older so I am taken seriously." Recently, I spoke with a former coworker, who is now a friend, about this. We both laughed as we threw our hands in the air and shrugged our shoulders in exasperation while lamenting in unison, "What is the right age?" We are either too young or too old. Are we ever at the right age? What is that age? I genuinely want to know.

And if you are an older worker, don't do this to the younger workers. Don't discriminate against them. Younger workers have just as much value as you.

Speak Up and Take a Stand

If you have yet to notice, a thread throughout this book is to speak up about the unspoken acts of discrimination, whether they are happening to you or someone else. Knowledge and awareness bring change. We must support each other by openly addressing the issues as they arise.

This especially holds true for the subject of the next chapter—racism. Even if you are not a person of color, to create a culture where discrimination of any kind does not exist, you must support each other, whether your affinity group or community is affected by that discrimination or not. Let's talk about how.

CLOSING THOUGHTS

Ageism in the tech industry is pervasive and often subtle, usually surfacing in hiring practices, work culture, and career advancement opportunities. While it may be difficult to prove, its impact leads to everything from exclusion to devalued experience to lost career opportunities. The best way to combat ageism is to stay ahead of it: remain adaptable, keep your skills sharp, and build a strong network.

- **Ageism starts early in tech.** With a median industry age of thirty-one, older professionals often face biases much sooner than in other fields.

- **Pay attention to subtle signs.** From dismissive interviewers to exclusion from key projects, age discrimination isn't always overt.

- **Stay relevant.** Continuously learning new technologies and skills can help combat biases about older workers being outdated.

- **Build a strong network.** Having connections in the industry can open doors and provide support if you face age-related challenges.

- **Speak up against ageism.** Whether advocating for yourself or others, addressing discriminatory remarks and policies can help evolve workplace culture.

Racism—When the Mask Slips

"I hear police sirens—they must be coming to arrest LeRon."

—LeRon L. Barton on a comment his coworkers made and
laughed about, quoted in *Harvard Business Review*

WE KNOW IT WILL HAPPEN EVENTUALLY; we find ourselves unconsciously waiting for it—in a group meeting, over a casual lunch, during after-work drinks, or even in a taxi ride to an event. At some point, people get comfortable, they drop their guard, and out come the racist comments and slurs. How you respond—whether the remark is aimed at you or not—ultimately depends on you.

My instinct is to call it out immediately, repeating what was said and making it clear that it was unacceptable. But as with most things, there's more to consider beyond just the immediate reaction. Let me share a story that illustrates exactly how this plays out in real life, with names changed for privacy.

"Let's take Tracy, for example, say she opens her own bubble tea shop," said "Larry."

He was directing this comment to "Tracy," an Asian woman on the marketing team, during a planning session. We were in the thick of the meeting, brainstorming ideas and letting the creative juices flow. Larry, my peer, was a dynamic guy with great experience. He often shared his expertise with the team, and these young professionals loved it. But as soon as he said this, the atmosphere in the room changed. I could feel the air leave the room. Larry's comment had made everyone uncomfortable.

People realized that Larry had just made a racist comment to a beloved team member. They were shocked by the remark and worried about Tracy, as they could feel her embarrassment and discomfort. I quickly had to decide whether or not I should stop the meeting and make sure Tracy was okay or keep the meeting going and not draw more attention to her. Two people on my team—Tracy's boss and one of her peers—did not hesitate. They immediately said, "That was offensive and out of line."

I announced that we were taking a fifteen-minute break. I spoke to Tracy and asked if she wanted to continue in the meeting—it was her choice. She was shaken but the consummate professional.

During the break, I also met with Larry. He said, "I knew it was wrong as soon as it came out of my mouth." He said he had passed a bubble tea shop on the way to work, and it stuck in his head. I told him he needed to apologize to Tracy. He agreed. I believe he apologized a day or so later. In the meantime, Tracy's boss took it to HR because another person on his team came forward and said that Larry had made a few other racist comments before this situation. I then had to speak to Larry and my boss.

My boss was angry. I have to say that when I saw his reaction to what happened, I breathed a small sigh of relief. I hadn't been sure what reaction I would get. I had too many experiences in the past where this was shrugged off as "people say things they shouldn't sometimes—no big deal." Or that look that they give you, like, *I don't want to deal with this* or *here we go again, another person claiming racism*. My boss did not do that. He addressed it with Larry, letting him know that it wasn't acceptable and he better not hear something like that again. I know this guy; I don't think he said it nicely. He was furious.

My boss and I knew nothing would happen to Larry, other than my boss addressing it, because Larry was acquainted with the CEO and good at his job. There was no way the company would lose that talent, and we all knew it.

But here is what I want to delve into regarding this situation: How do you work with someone after they have made racist comments at work?

Tracy's Reaction

When Larry made the comment, Tracy felt her face heat up. *Why me? Why single me out?* In that moment, she wasn't just Tracy, a teammate—she was being reduced to a stereotype. It was embarrassing and, honestly, disappointing. Larry was supposed to be a seasoned executive, someone who should know better. But there he was, making a comment that made everyone uncomfortable—especially her.

Tracy stayed in the meeting, not wanting to draw more attention to herself. No matter what, she would remain professional. But after the meeting, she felt alone. She knew her colleagues felt bad for her, but in reality, most of them would never fully understand what it was like to be on the receiving end of something like that. She found herself questioning—*Should I have said something? Should I just brush it off?* In the end, she decided to move on quickly, not for Larry's sake, but for her own.

He did apologize, but it was one of those apologies laced with justification, as if he was trying to explain it away. After that, Tracy didn't go out of her way to interact with him. If they had to work together, she kept it professional—strictly business. But any trust she had? Gone.[1]

Racism—Hiding in Plain Sight

Racism can come in many forms, from overt to unintentional, from obvious to subtle, and from clueless to cruel. It can also be overt *and* invisible at the same time, as relayed in the following story.

"Nicki" walked onto the floor on her first day on the job, the only person of color in a sea of young professionals whose faces were a mix of indifference and something colder. The tension in the air was immediate and heavy—almost palpable, like when you step into a room and the conversation suddenly stops.

She smiled, introduced herself, and made the small talk common to first-day conversations, but she did not receive warm responses from anyone.

She would walk in each morning and say, "Good morning." No one said it first. No one asked how her evening was. When she asked direct questions, they answered—but only just. No follow-up, no curiosity, no warmth. The rules of engagement were clear: Nicki wasn't one of them.

Conversations paused when she approached, only to resume when she walked past. Her colleagues spoke to each other with easy, effortless banter, laughing about weekend shenanigans and debating where to grab lunch. But they never looked her way. They never asked her to join.

At first, Nicki told herself it would change. That maybe they just needed time. A few days turned into weeks, and the silence never subsided. The message was there in what they didn't say and what they didn't do. She watched as invitations to lunch were extended freely in front of her—casual, instinctive, but never in her direction. She existed, but she wasn't included.

Nicki spoke to her manager about the situation, but this made her feel more isolated and alone. Racism is a difficult enough topic to discuss with your manager, especially if you are only one of two people of color on the floor. She assumed he would provide more concrete advice or even offer a solution such as, "Let's get you working on this project that will help you get to know the team on a different level." Or he could have been the change agent and invited Nicki out to lunch when they all talked about going to lunch together right in front of her—but he didn't do that.

After another month, he called Nicki into his office and told her it wasn't working out. He let her go without any severance. Nicki was out of work for two months without any pay, and she had a mortgage to pay and a family to support. Nicki said she had experienced racism at work before, but this, well, this was so blatant. They had let her know they didn't want her there. Nicki said she didn't understand why they had hired her in the first place.[2]

Nicki's story left me stunned. I have experienced racist remarks in every company where I've worked, and I have had people let me know how they felt about working with a person of color, but this was different. It wasn't one person; it was a group of people, and their behavior seemed intentional—they wanted her to know that she did not belong and they had no plans to welcome her into the company.

After that experience, Nicki became more discerning about the environments she worked in. This is an important takeaway for you. There are companies where you will never feel welcomed, but there are also companies with genuinely inclusive cultures. It's crucial to seek out those organizations and trust in your own worth. You will find a place where you can thrive in a culture that aligns with your values and where coworkers will speak up for you when you experience racism.

How to Determine If a Company Culture Aligns with Your Needs and Values

Finding the right company requires thorough research and thoughtful questions during the interview process. Here are key steps to help you evaluate whether a company's culture aligns with your needs and values.

Define what matters most to you.

Before evaluating a company, define your priorities. What aspects of company culture are nonnegotiable for you? Here are a few things to consider:

1. Work-life balance expectations
2. Leadership and management styles
3. Commitment to a fair and inclusive workplace
4. Growth and development opportunities

5. Company values and ethical standards

6. Remote work flexibility and policies

7. Team collaboration versus individual work

Research the company's public presence.

Once you know what's important to you, explore how the company presents itself and whether that aligns with your values.

1. **Company Website:** Review leadership bios and team pages. Are leadership roles diverse in gender, race, and background?

2. **LinkedIn & Social Media:** Check the company's posts, employee spotlights, and hiring announcements. Do they reflect an inclusive and supportive work environment?

3. **Job Descriptions:** Scan multiple job postings. Do they emphasize work-life balance and professional development? Or do they have rigid expectations (e.g., "We work hard and play hard" or "Must be from a top-tier school")?

4. **Press & News:** Look up articles about the company's culture, leadership, and employee experience.

Leverage employee insights.

1. **Glassdoor & Fishbowl:** Check CEO ratings, employee reviews, and salary transparency. Look for recurring themes in both positive and negative reviews.

2. **Former & Current Employees:** If you're replacing someone in the role, reach out to them on LinkedIn to understand

why they left. Connect with current employees, especially those from diverse backgrounds, to get their honest perspectives.

3. **Your Network:** Ask your colleagues if they've worked with or heard about the company. Reputations often spread within business circles.

Ask insightful questions during interviews.

Instead of asking generic culture questions, ask targeted, open-ended questions to get a real sense of the work environment. Note: Spread these questions throughout the conversation and ask different people during the interview process. It will feel more natural and less overwhelming.

1. **Leadership & Growth:**
   - How does leadership support employee growth and career development?
   - Can you share an example of someone who has grown significantly within the company?
   - How does the company handle feedback from employees? Can you give an example of a recent change made based on employee input?

2. **Diversity & Inclusivity:**
   - How does the company foster an inclusive environment for employees of different backgrounds?
   - What steps has leadership taken to promote diversity at all levels?

- Can you tell me about an employee resource group (ERG) or initiative that has made an impact?

3. **Work-Life Balance & Expectations:**

- How does the company define work-life balance? How is it supported in practice?

- What are the expectations around availability outside of regular work hours?

- Can you describe how the company supports employee well-being and mental health?

4. **Company Values in Action:**

- What are the company's core values, and how do they influence daily operations?

- Can you share a time when the company had to make a tough decision based on its values?

- What kind of behaviors and attitudes are most rewarded here?

5. **Team Dynamics & Communication:**

- How does the company foster collaboration among teams?

- Can you describe the communication style between leadership and employees?

- How are successes and failures handled within teams?

Evaluating a company for cultural fit is more than what is said in the interview. It is about aligning what a company says with what it actually does.

The Many Faces of Racism

Racism doesn't always look like slurs said in a planning session, as we saw with Tracy's story, or being obviously ignored, as we saw in Nicki's story. It's often not overtly codified in a work policy. More often, it's embedded in the culture—subtle but pervasive, protected and reinforced by those in power who prioritize the company's image and bottom line over accountability. Instead, it puts the burden of proof on those who experience the racist act. It appears in hiring processes, leadership behavior, and in the silence of those who claim to help but, in reality, fear rocking the boat. It forces on those of us who experience it the difficult decision of whether to speak out, endure, or walk away—each option carrying significant personal and professional costs.

> More often, racism is embedded in the culture—subtle but pervasive, protected and reinforced by those in power who prioritize the company's image and bottom line over accountability. Instead, it puts the burden of proof on those who experience the racist act.

The following stories illustrate how racism may show up for you at work, from an HR department that refuses to take responsibility for addressing racial slurs to a CEO openly expressing racist views. They show how leadership sets the tone for racism at work, how those in power often face no consequences, and how speaking up doesn't always garner the results you expect. Most importantly, these stories highlight that workplace racism isn't simply about the individual racist but about the culture and systems that allow it to persist.

Tackling Ethnic Slurs in the Workplace

One evening, ten of us—some coworkers and I—sat down for dinner. A few people from other regions were in town, such as South Africa, Australia, and the UK. During the dinner, I thought I heard someone sitting a few seats down from me use the word "nigger." At first, I doubted myself; it seemed too blatant, so I listened in more. Lo and behold, he used the word again—several times.

I was so shocked and angry (and embarrassed) that I was numb for the rest of the dinner. As the only person of color at the table, I felt uncomfortable addressing him there with all the other people. I left the dinner. I didn't get much sleep that night. I was tossing and turning, angry, and trying to decide whether to say something and to whom. Will they do anything about it?

I spoke to my boss. He was supportive and suggested that I speak to HR. He was a person of color too. I'm not sure I would have gone to him if he weren't; it would have been too uncomfortable. That is the problem—we take the burden off even the people we have to tell. Will it make them uncomfortable? We should not have to worry about that.

I spoke to an HR director. She asked me who was at the dinner and said she would look into it. I know she did because one coworker told me she called him. He said he didn't hear it, but he wasn't at that end of the table.

Shortly after that, she told me she wanted to meet with me and the person I claimed used this derogatory word so we could all discuss it. It was a very awkward meeting. We were in this big training room with rows of tables on risers. It felt odd and impersonal, so the HR director had us move some chairs down to the front of the classroom. We formed a triangle, so we were all facing each other. She stated why we were at the meeting.

Then she asked me to tell her what happened. I did. He denied it. I told him exactly what I heard him say. He then proceeded to tell us that he wasn't a racist and that he had plenty of Black friends back home in South Africa. Thankfully, the HR person jumped in and told him how insulting that was to say and that it didn't change what had happened. "She isn't here to hear how many Black friends you have," she said.

The conversation went round and round—with him denying he was a racist and me saying that I heard him use the word "nigger" several times. Clearly, others had heard it and confirmed it, or I don't think we would have been meeting. We weren't getting anywhere, and I said so. I didn't understand what the purpose of this was supposed to be. The HR director said, "You need to decide whether he should be fired."

My response was: "Why is the burden on me to choose? Doesn't the company have a policy against this? Shouldn't you be making that decision?"

She said it was my decision. I was furious. I felt like I was being insulted all over again. I told her I would not be making that decision. It wasn't mine to make. I did say that I wanted it in his employment record, and I did want his manager to know about this situation. The HR director told him that he would be fired immediately if it ever happened again.

I didn't walk away satisfied with the experience. I didn't feel supported or safe as a Black person in that company. She was too afraid to make the decision or didn't want to. Had the tables been turned—a White person making these claims against a Black person—would it have had the same outcome? Did she just run through these steps to say the company dealt with it? Those were the thoughts I had after the meeting.

I was younger then, but now I know I would have handled it differently. "Yes, I want him fired, and let's discuss how you, as a company, just handled this situation. Some policies and processes need to change." That would be my response now.

This wouldn't be the only time I spoke up about a racist situation to people who I thought would support me but also drive change. It didn't always turn out as I had envisioned.

Confronting Bigotry

I was interviewing for a job in NYC. I liked the hiring manager; he was very friendly, and I was excited about the prospect of living in the city again. As part of the interview process, I met with the CEO. During the interview, we somehow got on the subject of printing materials, and he made a derogatory comment about his printers, who were apparently of Indian descent. It started with "These Indians, they all . . ." and continued about how they rip everyone off, and it got worse from there. He did this several times. I was shocked and said something like, "Well, that might have been an isolated incident. Not all printers try to rip you off," or something to gently disagree with him and let him know he was stereotyping and making wide-sweeping generalizations. He didn't let it go. He repeated his comments.

I was angry and uncomfortable throughout the interview. This guy was arrogant, brash, domineering, and had no qualms about making racist comments. I knew then that I did not want to work for this man. Financially, I needed the job, but I didn't want it. I did not see myself working for him. I knew we didn't share values.

The interview finished, and by the time I returned to my hotel, the hiring manager called and said I had gotten the job and they wanted me to pick up my computer before I left the city. I picked up the computer, but everything in my being told me this wouldn't work out. I didn't feel good about this decision, but as I said, I needed the job.

On the drive back to Massachusetts, I was upset and furious and expressed my feelings to my husband. I knew I would not be happy working for the company because of the CEO, but I felt financially pressured to take the job.

Part of the interview process had included speaking with one of the principals at a well-known VC firm that backed this company. He had liked me; it had been a great interview. When he later called to ask me how my interview with the CEO went, I told him what had happened. He seemed appalled. He said all the right things— this was unacceptable, his company did not condone this behavior, he would speak to the CEO, et cetera, et cetera. I was happy that I told him. I thought *Okay, this is a great firm. They are going to deal with this situation.* The next day, I got a call from the CEO. He said, "Well, I guess this isn't going to work out."

I said, "No, it isn't." He then asked me to return the computer. That was it.

Racism Wrapped in Charity

Years later, I worked for a CEO who habitually bragged to the CRO, CFO, and me about his charity work and donations for kids. His stories were filled with racist views and derogatory statements about Black people. I would try to correct him, but he would go on and on about it. The CRO eventually pulled him aside and let him know my ethnicity. This only made it worse. He kept doing it. He would bring it up in meetings and hold us after meetings, and he started bragging about his charity work again, and out came his racist views.

It was so humiliating to have to sit there and listen to him talk about Black people—none of them could hold a job, they were lazy, they didn't have good families, they were uneducated, he hated rap music, and on and on he went. Even how he said the word "Blacks"— it was with such disdain.

I realized that I couldn't work for this man anymore. His racist views left me feeling nothing but contempt for him. This guy was so privileged that he was utterly clueless. His view of charity work was about helping people who should be grateful to him. His charity work allowed him to feel superior to others. I had no respect for him, and his ignorance was offensive. How could I let someone like that lead me? I started looking for another job and did my best to avoid situations that were not solely focused on work. As soon as we finished any meetings, I didn't linger and chitchat. I got up and walked out of the conference room.

My peers saved me as I was looking for new employment. We would openly talk about the CEO's lack of leadership skills, and we could even laugh about it. All of us were looking to leave. That support and camaraderie got me through until it was time to give my notice.

When I gave my notice, the CEO was upset. He didn't want me to leave, and he was nervous to tell the board I was going—not because he was worried about what I would say, but because an executive deciding to leave, one who was doing a good job, made him look bad. As soon as he told the board, one of the board members called me to ask why I was resigning. I told him. I told him because I knew he was in an interracial marriage, and he and I had engaged in many discussions on race in the past, so I felt comfortable with him. Otherwise, I don't know that I would have addressed the situation. I might have just left the company.

He was angry at the CEO and said that this behavior was unacceptable. A few days after I left, he called me and asked if I would share my experience with the chairman of the board. I said I would. This guy seemed to want to deal with this issue. I spoke to the chairman. He apologized for the behavior and said it was unacceptable; he would deal with it.

It changed nothing.

These experiences left me feeling profoundly depressed and exasperated. I became disenfranchised by the tech industry. I considered leaving the industry many times, but I realized racism is everywhere, and this was the industry that I knew and enjoyed. My experience was in software, and it would be challenging to switch industries because of how much time I had already spent in tech. So, I've remained in this industry. I wrote this book because I don't want any of you to feel what I felt at that time. It was a low in my life. I truly felt lost. I want you to feel supported and validated and give you the tools to address these situations as they arise so you can come out of them with less emotional turmoil than I or those who shared their stories with me did.

Assumptions Breed Contempt

The reality is that we often experience racism from coworkers when they are letting down their guard. Sometimes it shows up in the middle of a casual dinner, masked as curiosity or a joke, and can happen to anyone—even from people of the same race—but the impact is just as harmful. Let me tell you about a former employee, now a friend of mine.

A few of us went out to dinner together, and across the table, I noticed one of my team members was visibly upset. "Brooke" was sitting in the corner with another employee, one who didn't report to me but was part of our department. Voices were slightly raised, and the look on Brooke's face was a mix of disgust, shame, and anger. Everyone's body language conveyed that it was a heated discussion and that the other employee and his boss were ganging up on her and enjoying it.

Later that evening, as we walked back to our hotel, Brooke confided in me and a few others about what had happened. She grew up in South Africa and is a White South African. During dinner, a White male colleague from the UK asked her if she had owned slaves after learning where she was from. He went on to make broad claims that most White South Africans were racists. His boss joined in, agreeing with him, reinforcing the insinuation that she was racist. Some of it was disguised as jokes and other times they were making bold statements of racism.

Brooke was so upset and embarrassed that this conversation had happened, that it had been her coworker and an executive, and that it had been in front of her other peers. She spent the entire dinner defending herself against a racial slur she had heard too many times in her life. She was relatively new to the company, and it left a lasting stain on her perception of the work culture.

The situation was made worse when Larry (who made the bubble tea comment) joined in, reinforcing the racist remarks instead of correcting his employee. When Brooke reported the incident to HR—along with Larry's bubble tea comment—she hoped it would lead to corrective action. It did not.

In that exchange, Brooke was not just being questioned about owning slaves, she was being accused. She was reduced to a stereotype about South Africans and forced to defend herself against assumptions she had no control over. According to Brooke, it wasn't the first time she had been stereotyped as a racist South African, but having it happen in a professional setting added to the insult and feelings of isolation.

Getting Past a Racist Comment

This is where decisions come in. I had to continue to work with Larry because our jobs required it. I could have reduced the interaction with him and cooled our working relationship. I chose not to. The success of our teams relied heavily on our relationship and collaboration. It was important to me that we maintained a strong rapport, despite his deplorable behavior. As a leader, I knew it was important to model professionalism and remain focused on the shared goals of the team. By doing so, I helped the team remain productive while setting an example of how to rise above adverse situations.

Throughout your career, you will work with many people who have racist or biased views. The goal is not to excuse or tolerate racism while maintaining your professionalism and moving forward. Stay focused on what you are trying to accomplish—growing your career.

How and When to Speak Up

As Tracy's coworkers did, speak up if you witness someone making racist or derogatory comments to a coworker. We must promote an inclusive work environment and let people know that anything else is unacceptable. Supporting someone when a situation happens is incredibly helpful to that person. They may be in shock and unable to respond immediately, as my female colleague was when the CEO kept talking over her. Or they may feel uncomfortable speaking out in front of others. They may not know whether others will support them.

You will need to make decisions when these situations happen. If they are blatant, then getting HR involved is a good idea. Of course, you may be aware of the time a coworker did go to HR but nothing came of it. But consider a situation where you're unlikely to get any kind of positive outcome, which is what happened to me when two of my complaints involved CEOs.

Most companies are not going to get rid of a CEO for making racist comments to one person. They just aren't. If it happens to many people and you take the legal route, the company may remove the CEO, but that is a complicated process.

Still, I think getting HR involved is important because it puts the person and the company on notice that you and others will speak up when racism occurs. They may investigate, and the person may or may not be removed from their position, but it goes on record that there was an issue. If it continues with that person or if there are other situations in the company, it is now recorded that there were past incidents.

And remember: Racism, like other forms of discrimination, is against the law. Title VII of the Civil Rights Act of 1964 protects employees against racism, including harassment that involves racial slurs, offensive remarks, or displays of racially offensive symbols.[3]

As I wrote earlier, racism isn't going away, but this is about making decisions when it occurs. Here are some steps you can take if you experience or witness (also important) racism at work:

1. **Acknowledge what happened to you.** And don't doubt yourself. Reflect on how the comment affected you.

2. **Document the situation as soon as possible.** This includes the date, time, place, and what was said. Document everything from the initial situation to addressing it with the person and seeking help from HR. Blind copy everything to your personal email account. This is good to have in case it continues; you have a record of everything, and it shows you tried to address the issue.

3. **Decide whether you want to confront the person.** Only do so if you feel safe. When confronting, restate what they said to you, ask them what they meant by it, and tell them how it made you feel. Set boundaries with them. It is not your obligation to educate someone else on the impact of racist comments, but if you typically have a good rapport with this person and feel they will be open to hearing what you have to say, then explain why it was offensive and the impact of such comments.

4. **Remain professional.** When it happens, confront the person, speak to HR, and always remain professional. As a person of color, you know you will be judged on how you handle a situation. You don't want anything to cloud the act of racism. You want the focus on the situation, not on you. Going in with a ton of anger, raising your voice, and showing too much frustration won't help the situation. You can say you are angry without showing anger. You can say you are frustrated without showing frustration. You can calmly state the seriousness of the situation and express your expectations on how it will be handled.

I have learned to smooth out my responses to situations, always remaining calm and objective. It doesn't mean I don't express my feelings. I do, but without emotion. It shows leadership and professionalism. Don't give them what they expect to see because if you do, it allows them to focus on you versus the racist situation that they more than likely don't want to address.

5. **Get HR involved.** If confronting the person doesn't resolve the issue or if you don't feel comfortable addressing the person directly, go to your HR department.

6. **Get support from friends, colleagues, and your network.** Seek professional help if it impacts your mental well-being.

7. **Monitor the situation.** If it happens again, document it and report it to HR. If HR doesn't help to resolve the problem or if the environment becomes intolerably hostile, like the case of Owen Diaz at Tesla, consider exploring legal action.

Racist Behavior Is Not a Reflection on You

I shared a few stories of my experience and others with you, but they are precisely that—a few. Let's not overlook the fact that there are millions more. As many of you know, this happens a lot at work, at conferences, or out for drinks. It can and does happen at any time. We subconsciously ready ourselves for it. Steel ourselves. Brace ourselves. It is exhausting. Day after day, year after year.

Racism is something we have to contend with in the corporate world. You can make decisions about where you want to work, and there may be companies that genuinely don't tolerate racism at any level. I just haven't found one.

You also can make decisions about what you will and will not accept, what you will speak up about, how you will support others when you see that they are being mistreated because of their race, and how you will work with people who you know have racist views.

Most importantly, you can decide how you react—internally and externally—to people when these situations arise. They are racist; they are ignorant. This is not a reflection on you.

It's important to be aware of other forms of racism, such as subtle microaggressions, which can also be based on gender, culture, and beliefs. These verbal slights, intentional or otherwise, communicate hostile, derogatory, or negative attitudes. In the next chapter, we delve into microaggressions, providing examples from personal experiences and strategies for addressing them.

CLOSING THOUGHTS

Racism in the workplace is a harsh reality for many of us, whether it be subtle (being excluded) or blatant. Regardless of its degree, the impact can be isolating and demoralizing. However, how you react in these moments matters for your well-being, career, and the push for cultural change. Some workplaces will never be truly inclusive. Know your worth and seek companies where you feel respected. And remember that racism in the workplace is against the law.

- **Decide whether to address it directly.** If you feel safe, restate what was said, ask for clarification, and articulate why you found it unacceptable.

- **Document everything.** Keep records of incidents, including dates, times, locations, and what was said.

- **Stay professional.** How you respond matters, especially as a person of color. Express your frustration but remain composed. Don't let your reaction become the focus instead of the racist act itself.

- **Speak up for others.** Sometimes the person targeted by the comment is too shocked to respond or may worry that others agree with the perpetrator. Speaking up is important to show that the behavior is unacceptable and the victim is supported.

Microaggressions— It's the Little Things

"'So, I thought affirmative action was over. How'd you get here?' 'He thought it was funny,' she said."

—Sandra McPherson, as quoted in an NBC news article

THERE ARE THE COMMON MICROAGGRESSIONS marginalized people experience and hear about: questions about where we are from, curiosity about our hair, comments about how we speak, what we eat, who we love, or how we worship. Like racism, microaggressions are endless, so much so that 97 percent of minorities said they preferred remote work because they felt they could avoid these interactions at work.[1]

The data show that microaggressions are common in the workplace. A survey conducted by *Fortune* and SurveyMonkey in 2019 showed that 60 percent of respondents have experienced or witnessed a microaggression.[2]

Earlier, we defined microaggressions as statements, actions, or incidents regarded as instances of indirect, subtle, or unintentional discrimination against members of a marginalized group, such as a racial or ethnic minority. Microaggressions can be grouped into any of these categories: race/ethnicity/nationality, gender identity, sexual orientation, religion, age, socioeconomic status, disability, or neurodiversity.

Microaggressions Under the Microscope

I heard from "Tamara" about a situation that was disturbing and highlights how easily microaggressions used in the workplace are dismissed as harmless yet create lasting impact and can diminish the perception of the person. Tamara received an email from "Richard," a coworker. Without speaking to Tamara first, Richard emailed Tamara and a client and said that Tamara could finish this task by such-and-such date. The work described in the email was Richard's responsibility, not Tamara's. Tamara confronted him and let him know that it was his responsibility, not hers, and she would not complete the task. Tamara was professional—calm and matter-of-fact—when she discussed this with him.

Richard, however, escalated the situation to HR, forcing Tamara to meet with her direct manager and Richard about the incident. The conversation quickly moved away from the reason for the meeting and moved to how she walked down the hallway. Richard told her she walked aggressively down the hallway and with a mean face—like a bitch. He said he didn't know how to approach her when she walked down the hallway. Tamara asked if he expected her to smile whenever she walked down a hallway, always considering her facial expression. Tamara's boss responded to this exchange by asking Tamara, "How could we fix this?"

At the start of my conversation with Tamara, she shared an observation about a White woman in the company, "Mary," who frequently would rudely and aggressively push back on leadership in meetings, often slamming her hands down on the table. Despite her aggressive behavior, people accepted it. Mary was White, and Tamara was Black.[3]

You might think this is a case of racism—and it is—but the microaggression lies in the way Richard portrayed Tamara as aggressive and angry. Was this an instance of unconscious bias, or did Richard make these statements to undermine Tamara in front of her boss? Or perhaps both?

Regardless of intent, these comments are harmful. They reinforce damaging stereotypes about Black people being angry and aggressive, not to mention the sexist assumption that women should walk around with smiling faces so as to please their male coworkers. This is especially true for women of color, creating a double burden. This kind of labeling can have serious consequences, both for the individual and the work environment.

So what did Tamara do? She immediately started job hunting and left the company a few months later.

It's a Fine Line . . .

There are two types of microaggressors I have encountered: biased and clueless.

The first person is clearly racist, homophobic, or sexist but understands that racism (along with the other -isms) are generally frowned upon. Therefore, these people can't openly share their views at work without risk, so they take the safer path of expressing their opinions more subtly with microaggressions. Their ability to backtrack when they get called out for their comment provides a greater degree of deniability. They can claim to have been misunderstood or that you—the person attacked—are just being too sensitive. This allows space for the microaggressor, and they can create a situation whereby your anger or frustration makes you look like the smaller person—the complainer, the whiner.

There is such a fine line with microaggressions; deliberate practitioners know how to use this to their advantage. This chapter's epigraph is a good example. This type of microaggressor is more dangerous than the other class, which I'll call the clueless class.

The racist microaggressors are more dangerous because they use these slights to show disdain for a particular group. They show their perceived superiority by freely expressing their opinions without the risk of reprimand. The clueless folks say things without understanding the implications of what they said. It often stems from small talk, curiosity, and—of course—ignorance.

Because microaggressions can be construed as casual remarks, they often go unaddressed. Microaggressions are easily defended by claiming you, the target, are being overly sensitive and should just brush it off; this is coupled with the current social climate that portrays many as being hypersensitive, adding to cancel culture, and leaning too far into political correctness.

When these issues are addressed, the response can often take on another form called a secondary microaggression. These include "gaslighting" (the perpetrator tries to convince you that the racist comment was not racist, contextualizing it as a joke like we see in this chapter's epigraph), victim-blaming (faulting you for your reaction to the microaggression), or someone else speaking for the microaggressor to smooth it over (they try to explain what the offender "meant" to say). There is also the case where a microaggression happens, and those who witness it don't say anything. They don't speak up or support the victim.

Any of these can leave you questioning yourself and feeling alienated from your coworkers.

In this chapter, I share some examples of microaggressions I have experienced or that have been shared with me. I talk about how it feels in the moment and the lasting impacts, how I have addressed situations that I experienced, and ways you can address people and related considerations. My goal in sharing, as always, is to give voice to what many of us are experiencing, to help you feel supported in your experience, and to provide you with tools and words to work through these situations. These will help you thrive despite these occurrences of bias and discrimination.

Let's start with some common microaggressions.

"What Are You?"

We sat at the round tables on our floor, eating lunch. I was a new employee, and a few coworkers had asked me to join them. We were having the typical lunchroom conversation. The conversations were not isolated to each table; we were talking across tables.

One of the people I was sitting with asked me where I was from. Everyone got really interested in the conversation—all eyes were on me. I said Massachusetts.

They said, "No, I mean, where are you really from?"

I said, "Massachusetts."

"No," they said, "I mean, what are you?"

"What do you mean, what am I?" I said. "I am a human, just like you."

"No, you don't look like you're from here," another person said. So where are you from?"

"Massachusetts," was all I could say. The room got quiet, and everyone seemed uncomfortable. I changed the subject, and we all moved on.

Imagine being the only person of color in a room and getting asked that question—over and over again. Well, I am sure some of you don't have to imagine it because you have more than likely experienced it as many times as I have.

Another time, I was in my office with an employee. I was new to the company and had only been there a few weeks. We were discussing campaigns. Out of nowhere, this person asked me where I was from and said "we" were just curious. Apparently, she was asking for the team. We went from discussing campaign results to my background within seconds. My response: "Does it matter?"

"Well, no, but . . ."

"Good. Let's move on."

I didn't always approach this situation the way I just described. When I was younger it made me uncomfortable to make others uncomfortable. I would stumble over my response and say that my father is American and my mother is German. But the questions wouldn't stop—they wanted to know where my father was from in America. They needed me to say that I was Black. Even though they knew I was not White. They needed me to say it.

But I was at work, trying to do my job. This line of questioning was and is inappropriate and unnecessary. I got tired of answering these questions.

My responses now are structured to enlighten the person asking about the inappropriateness of their questions. I want them to think about what they are asking and, more importantly, *why* they are asking it. It isn't pertinent information for what we try to accomplish at work. I am not here to feed your curiosity. I am not a subject to be researched or explored.

If you aren't a person of color and are wondering why this is so offensive, ask yourself, as a White American, how many times you have been asked this question. When asked this question, I am singled out from the rest of the people in that room or at that company. It becomes a loaded question with lots of implicit views on race, ethnicity, and the stereotypes that are linked to them.

> But the questions wouldn't stop. They needed me to say that I was Black. Even though they knew I was not White. They needed me to say it.

We already feel singled out in an environment where there are few—if any—who look like us. When this happened to me, I was the only person of color in that room and in the entire company. I have never been asked that question when there were other minorities in the room. When you ask this question, you tell me you see me as different from the norm and that I don't seem to belong here—I am "othered" in a way that no one else is, as if my presence requires extra explanation or justification.

I spoke with one woman who told me she often gets asked where she is from. When she says Massachusetts, they say, "No, where are you really from? You have an accent." I had to laugh when she told me this. This woman sounds like she is from Massachusetts. She has a slight Boston accent. Yet, because she is a Black woman with a lighter skin tone, they assume she is from some Caribbean island, and they even "hear" a Caribbean accent.

This is an excellent example of unconscious bias—when we unconsciously hold certain beliefs and stereotypes about a particular group of people, so much so that we hear or see something that isn't even there.

These biases easily slip into our conversations. It's not always intentional, but it sure feels like it to the person on the receiving end. It alienates us in an environment where we should all be focused on performing the job we were hired to do. But we are always consciously or unconsciously on alert for these situations, steeling ourselves for it because we know it will happen; we just don't know when.

Do You Want That Straight or Curly?

Should we move on to hair? Right now, I can hear people of color saying, "Oh boy, here we go." That's right, we are going there. We must discuss this. Why? Because of the obvious and blatant racism and sheer ignorance that hair-related microaggressions showcase and the magnitude of the problem.

If you aren't a woman of color and you have never experienced this, you may think that just because someone may feel slighted, doesn't make it true. That it's simply their insecurity.

But these microaggressions around hair happen so frequently that in 2019, California passed a law against them. And other states followed suit. As of 2024, twenty-four of the fifty US states have enacted this law.

The CROWN Act was created in 2019 by the CROWN Coalition, founded by Dove, in partnership with California state Senator Holly Mitchell. CROWN stands for Creating a Respectful and Open

World for Natural hair. Its purpose is to ensure protection against discrimination based on race-based hairstyles and hair textures—braids, locs, twists, and knots—in the workplace and in public schools.[4]

Can we stop for a second and absorb the absurdity of the need for a law that is required to protect someone against discrimination at work (and school) because of their hair? How demeaning can this get?

It is absurd, but it is a real issue, as the following stats from the Crown 2023 Workplace Research Study, a joint effort by Dove and LinkedIn, illuminate.[5]

- Black women with coiled or textured hair are twice as likely to experience microaggressions at work than Black women with straight hair.

- Over 20 percent of Black women between the ages of twenty-five and thirty-four have been sent home from work because of their hair.

- Among Black women, 25 percent believe they have been denied a job because of their hair.

- Two-thirds of Black women change their hair for a job interview, and 41 percent of them change their hair from curly to straight.

- Up to 54 percent of Black women feel they have to wear their hair straight to an interview for it to be successful.[6]

I get asked about my hair a lot at work. I get questions whether I'm wearing it curly or straight or back in a ponytail, even though many women, White women included, wear their hair in different styles based on their desire, their outfit, the weather, or how much time they had that morning to get ready for work.

The "many hairstyles of Kae." If I had a dollar for every time I have heard that comment . . . This type of curiosity shows a discomfort with anyone who isn't White and illustrates predetermined views of what hair texture and style should be—what is acceptable and what is professional. Even if I wear my hair straight, I am not like them in their eyes. My hair is unlike theirs, and they can't seem to grasp that everyone's hair texture, including theirs, is unique.

The typical situation for me, and it has happened many times, is this:

Them: How do you get your hair straight?

Me: I blow-dry it.

Them: No, I mean, do you use a straightener or something to get it straight?

Me: No, I blow-dry it. Why are you asking me this?

Them: A blow dryer can't get your hair that straight.

Me: I just told you that I blow-dried it straight.

If I continue the conversation, although I typically don't, I respond like this: "Is your hair perfectly straight, or does it have a curl or wave? Many people don't have perfectly straight hair, so they blow-dry it like I do. How relevant is my hair to our work?" Then they stumble, stumble, and stumble again over their words.

But of course, when I do that, I know in their eyes that now I am an angry Black woman to be avoided or who they need to walk on eggshells around. This creates an unfair burden on those being discriminated against, forcing them to navigate constant emotional and psychological stress, diminishing their sense of self-worth while enduring the unfair challenge of proving their value in environments that often marginalize or overlook them.

Strange Things We've Heard at Work

This is why we often ignore microaggressions: If we respond the way we want to, the way we have a right to, we will be viewed as threatening. Even though the questions that we are asked are threatening to us. We are singled out as being different. We are not the norm. We are not acceptable in their eyes.

"Yours looks messy and frizzy."

This was "Elena's" feedback on her presentation. To be clear, the presentation topic was not about hair but graphic design. Elena was presenting to a senior professional, along with six other people. After each person presented, the professional would offer feedback about the presentation. That's when she told Elena her hair looked messy and frizzy. The rest of the input for Elena was: "You need to make sure your hair looks more professional."

Elena told me she did not know how to respond. She was in shock. Up until that moment, she had respected this senior professional's experience. This comment was made in front of those six other people. This woman might as well have said to Elena, "Your ethnicity isn't professional or appropriate."

When Elena relayed this story to me, she said, "My hair is curly, not frizzy." She was explaining *her hair*. We should not have to justify our hair. It hurt to hear her say it. It hurt to understand that she felt the need to defend her hair.

We discussed our experiences with this and other microaggressions, and what Elena said when I asked her how it made her feel stuck with me. She said, "It immediately brought me back to when I was four years old and experienced racism for the first time. I was that four-year-old girl all over again. It wasn't a kid bullying me at school; this was a grown woman well-established in her career."[7]

How can you ever prepare for that?

Even after we have experienced it many times and are unconsciously prepared for it, it is still shocking and painful when it happens. That is the impact an act of a racist microaggression has. It carries so much more weight than that single microaggression. It affects us for a long time, adds to our collection of bad experiences, and recalls past experiences, as we heard from Elena. They pile up day after day, year after year. They make us reassess ourselves in light of someone else's view of what makes us unique. The judgment of who we are, the statement that we are not enough because of something we have no control over, is considered unacceptable. Microaggressions say that Elena's curly hair is not as good as "Sandy's" straight hair. And if we fight back and confront the person, they say: "You are making a big deal about nothing."

It is infuriating, egregious, and exhausting. It must stop. We must address it when it happens and support others when we witness it. When I am faced with this question, the approach that works best for me is to ask, "How is it relevant for you to know about my hair at work?"

Here are some more doozies I've heard at work, and brief explanations as to why they're so atrocious.

"You Can Speak Proper English?"

This young guy came into the office for an interview. I was part of the interview process. He and I had a great conversation. I thought he was a good fit for the role, was easy to get along with, and would fit in with the rest of the team. He got a thumbs-up from me. After the interviews were over, my boss and I discussed the candidates. When we got to this candidate, my boss said several times, "He is so articulate. Man, he is just so articulate." His voice conveyed surprise, as if it's unusual for a Black person to be articulate. We hired this man, and after he gave a presentation, I heard another senior person say the same thing with the same amount of surprise. "Michael is SO articulate."

Now, I have had people say to me that I was articulate. I have had people say that I am a great communicator. There are times when this is said as a compliment and times when it is said with shock and awe. Intent—it matters. You must determine the intent behind the words in some of these situations. Not all are slights, and not all are compliments.

My response to this, if it isn't meant as a compliment, is to say, "You seem surprised that I am articulate, why is that?" These situations call for directness. Softening the blow just gives them an easy out. Your response must be impactful. You want the person to stop and think about what they are saying or implying and hopefully never do it again.

"Why Don't You Sound Black?"

Pre-COVID and Zoom calls, my new-hire interview process started with a phone call followed by an in-person interview. I interviewed one candidate via phone. He had good experience, and we had good rapport on the call. I decided he was a possible candidate for the role and asked him to come in for an in-person interview.

He was in the conference room before I was. I came into the

room, tried to shake his hand, and introduced myself, and I realized how flustered he was. He said, "Oh when I spoke to you on the phone, I didn't realize you were . . . you sounded different on the phone." He couldn't complete his sentences. I knew he was shocked that I was a person of color because I didn't "sound Black."

He was so uncomfortable. I could tell he didn't want to finish the interview. He could barely answer the questions. I remained professional and conducted the interview. Later that day, an HR director told me that when they followed up with the candidate, he told them I was very intimidating, and he didn't think he could work for me.

I have had people at work say to me "You don't sound Black" when they find out my race and ethnicity. My response: "How does Black sound?" And that's where the stumbling starts.

"Hey, Man, What's Happenin'?"

During an offsite planning, "Daniel," a new salesperson in the company, shared some of his thoughts on a subject. Daniel was a person of color. A White salesperson repeatedly responded to Daniel's ideas with replies such as "Hey, bro, that's cool" and raised his hand to give high fives. His behavior stood out to everyone in the room because he never addressed any White people that way, in the room or at any other time at work. He did not recognize Daniel's ideas with the same professional respect as others. He may have felt that this approach would make Daniel feel like a part of the group, but it had the opposite effect.

This was a microaggression. Rather than treating Daniel as an equal, he highlighted Daniel's ethnicity, showing he viewed Daniel differently than his other peers. Daniel was different and, therefore, needed to be addressed differently. This guy didn't think he could speak to Daniel in a professional manner like he did with others. This behavior undermined Daniel's professional contributions and reinforced a bias that people of color should be engaged with differently in a professional setting.

I would address this behavior in the room by asking them their intention: "Do you mean to speak to me in slang, or is your intention to address me differently than you do everyone else in the room? The 'hey bro's' and the high fives? Are you aware that you are showing bias and disrespect to me right now?" Hit it head-on.

Again, it is important that your response is impactful, because you want to bring awareness to their microaggression and bias. People's biases run so deep that many are unaware of what they are doing, though in a moment, we discuss people who are very aware of this and examine why they use microaggressions. Before we do, here is a recent example of the extreme nature of bias that can happen at any time.

In the July 1, 2024, *CBS Mornings* segment, Jericka Duncan interviewed cofounders Earl Cooper and Olajuwon Ajanaku about their company, Eastside Golf. As they conducted an on-course interview about how their brand is breaking barriers in the sport by making golf more accessible and inclusive, especially for people of color, the interview was interrupted by other golfers asking them if they were shooting a music video.

Another example is a statement that President Donald Trump made at a debate during the 2024 US presidential election cycle where he referred to "Black jobs" (referring to lower-paying jobs) being taken away by immigrants. He insinuated that Black people hold only lower-level jobs.

"They're taking Black jobs now and it could be 18, it could be 19 and even 20 million people," former President Donald Trump said in the debate Thursday about the role immigrants play in the U.S. economy. "They're taking Black jobs, and they're taking Hispanic jobs, and you haven't seen it yet, but you're going to see something that's going to be the worst in our history."[8]

This exchange highlights the persistent stereotyping and deep-rooted biases that only people of color occupy lower-level (also meaning lower-paying) jobs. President Trump never mentioned White people in this exchange.

Is My Seniority Good or Bad?

In Chapter 5, we discussed ageism. Of course, there are microaggressions related to ageism. Though ageism is typically associated with older workers, it can also happen to younger workers.

As I have progressed through my career, I have fallen victim to common microaggressions for the "older worker." Comments like, "You are so senior" or "You are the most seasoned of the team." I have also seen this during interview processes when the under-thirty HR representative looks at your resume and says, "You seem overqualified for this role." That always struck me as odd—how can you be overqualified? You are qualified, or you are not qualified.

We hear things like: "That is the old way of doing things; things are different now. Let one of the younger people on your team figure that out; they are better at technology."

". . . Than you are" is the part of that sentence they are leaving out.

And then we hear the exact opposite, which happens to younger workers: "This was way before your time. We figured this out long before you did; you don't have enough experience to understand real business decisions."

Addressing ageist microaggressions can be challenging, as ageism typically is delivered subtly. However, asking clarifying questions can help to bring attention to what they are saying and how you are receiving their comments. "Are you concerned that I don't have enough experience for [x]? You've mentioned my seniority several times. How are my years of experience a hindrance?"

Microaggressions Take a Toll

We all work in environments with conscious and unconscious biases streaming in and out of our days. Microaggressions can and do happen to anyone, no matter their background, gender, or level. They are often verbal, but they can be nonverbal as well. I have had people stare at me with utter disdain at work, letting me know that I am not welcome and they don't want to work with me. I've had people not want to sit next to me in a meeting and heard them make fun of someone else's accent or insist they can't understand an accent without truly trying. We all do it, sometimes unintentionally and other times intentionally. Either way, it must be addressed. Leaving it unaddressed allows the microaggressions to continue.

Most of the acts of discrimination discussed in this book take both an emotional and a physical toll. Studies have shown the impact these actions make on a person's health. Having to experience sexism, racism, and microaggressions year after year causes depression, sleep deprivation, anxiety, and high blood pressure, to name just a few ailments. Discrimination causes stress, and stress leads to health issues.[9]

According to an article in *Harvard Business Review*, it takes such a toll that as people started going back to the office after COVID-19, only 3 percent of Black professionals were ready to go back to work versus 21 percent of White professionals.[10] One of the reasons cited was that remote work provided a respite from microaggressions. I get that. I agree with that. Though remote work doesn't protect us entirely from them. I still experience microaggressions on Zoom calls, but the format allows me to step away when needed. It gives me some breathing room.

Working remotely helps me keep my work and the people I work with in perspective. I have a healthier balance of the importance of their thoughts and opinions in my life and my view of myself.

How Best to Respond?

As you can see, the impact of these statements is real and lasting, and we are once again faced with the decision of whether to address it, and if so, how best to do that. This is a crucial moment of empowerment and responsibility. You must decide: Do I play along? Do I educate? Do I ignore it?

How should we respond to a microaggression? I already gave you a few examples of how I responded in the past or how I would respond now. It isn't easy and it's often uncomfortable, but creating an inclusive environment demands that we address microaggressions as they arise.

There are a few things to consider when addressing these comments. Think about these now so that you have a plan for reacting when faced with this. In the moment, we can be taken aback and shocked, and we don't always respond how we would like. And that's okay. You can always go back and address it.

Determine the Intent

What was the intent behind the comment? Was it intentionally used to make you feel singled out, less-than? We discussed the two types of microaggressors. Is yours the one who is purposely hiding behind this microaggression because it is more defendable than a direct racist or sexist comment? Or is this person clueless as to the impact the remark has?

Typically you will be able to tell which type of microaggressor you are dealing with by what they say and how they say it. We'll identify the first group as those who know what they're doing and mean to offend. Their comments will be intentional, more jarring, and close to a blatant act of sexism, racism, etc. These people want a reaction out of you. You may have witnessed this behavior from them before.

On the other hand, if a comment comes from someone who is clueless, it will be more innocent and, frankly, ignorant. You will sense that they are stating their opinion or saying something quickly without having thought through what they just said.

If it is the former, the intentional, I would respond at that moment. You can ask them if they meant that statement to be racist, sexist, or whatever it is. I would ask this calmly and coming from a place of curiosity rather than being accusatory. And then you can tell them the comment is unacceptable. If they continue with these comments, I'd report it to HR because they are clearly creating a hostile work environment.

If you're dealing with someone who doesn't realize the impact, you have a choice to make. You can address it right away, which is what I would do if I were alone with this person. Or if you're in front of a crowd, you might want to consider speaking to them privately. It all depends on what was said, the impact, and how others reacted at that moment—like when I was in the cafeteria being asked about my background, and everyone at the table wanted to know.

Sometimes in a crowd, you can say, "That was inappropriate" and move on. You have to judge quickly whether the person will be combative. If you feel comfortable dealing with someone who might get combative, then go ahead and address it head-on. But if not, then take the person aside. Remember that in these situations, we are often left being the one viewed as confrontational or angry. That doesn't mean you shouldn't address it, but you should consider your approach.

Always Remain Professional

I stay professional, but short and to the point, when I deal with these issues. I am cuttingly clear in my response. I say it with authority and strength but always calmly.

Consider your relationship with this person. Is this someone you enjoy working with and know well? Is this someone you must work with and maintain a good relationship with? If you think yes to either of these questions, then pulling them aside and letting them know their comment was inappropriate might be enough. If you don't know them and this relationship doesn't matter to you or your work, you can choose to ignore it—the first time it happens. But if it happens again, you should address it, or you could pull them aside and tell them they were being inappropriate.

Be prepared to explain why it was inappropriate. This can be tricky. If it is the aggressive and intentional microaggressor we discussed and they ask this question, you can be sure they are headed to "you are too sensitive," "you took it the wrong way," or "you are overreacting." If that happens, I would state why their comment was inappropriate, tell them they know it was unacceptable, and then end the discussion by saying, "I was clear on why that was inappropriate, and this conversation is over."

What if it is your manager or a senior person? What do you do then? Well, that depends on the severity of the comment and the intent. If it is severe and the purpose was to belittle or single out, then you can speak to them directly or go to HR (or someone senior in the company you feel supported by) and have them help you address it with the person.

If it wasn't intentional and simply an ignorant statement, you can say it was inappropriate and leave it at that. Or, depending on your relationship with your boss, you can pull them aside or wait until your next one-on-one meeting and say, "I wanted to talk to you about a comment you made yesterday that made me feel really uncomfortable, and I thought it was inappropriate." You can also say, "Hey, I am sure you didn't mean it the way it came out, but what you said yesterday was potentially problematic."

If you decide you can't address it with this person because it could jeopardize your job, there is no judgment here. There will be times when you choose to keep quiet to preserve your financial well-being and career. That is okay. You aim to succeed in your career and get more open-minded people in higher-level positions to create more inclusive work environments. Again, there is no judgment.

There are so many types of microaggressions—race, gender, sexual, religious, disabilities, neurodiversity, and class. They happen all the time. We can all fall victim to them, although they are predominantly directed at marginalized groups. They can be intentional and unintentional. Either way, they significantly impact us: They single us out as different. They take something about us and make it unacceptable, against the norm. Less-than. They are called microaggressions, but the impact is at a macro level.

Speak Up for Others, Especially If You're a Leader

We can do our part by addressing microaggressions as they happen to us or if we witness them. Supporting victims of microaggressions by speaking out can have a more substantial impact than if the victim speaks out themselves. Others speaking out for the person shows the aggressor that it is unacceptable to others, not just the marginalized person.

Microaggressions can define a work culture if left unaddressed. My general approach is to ask a question like "How does Black sound?" In so doing, I enlightened the perpetrator of their bias and ignorance. It can work, depending on the transgressor. If they are using it to express their bigoted views and shield themselves from harsh sanctions, enlightenment doesn't always work.

That is why leadership must be front and center to condemn this behavior. They play a critical role in resolving this issue in the workplace. Some leaders are champions of an inclusive work culture, and I have worked for several. However, some leaders, knowingly or unknowingly, can create a culture of exclusivity where things like microaggressions can thrive. We discuss how to work with these ego-first leaders in the next chapter.

CLOSING THOUGHTS

Microaggressions are not just harmless remarks; they reflect the biases we have discussed in this book. They shape the culture and perpetuate workplace discrimination. Whether intentional or unintentional, microaggressors contribute to an environment where marginalized individuals feel othered, scrutinized, and excluded. Because calling out microaggressions is often dismissed as "woke," oversensitive, or being politically correct, they frequently go unchallenged and reinforce systemic inequities. Addressing them requires awareness and action—calling them out, educating others, and fostering a safe and respectful workplace where everyone is genuinely included.

- **Microaggressions take two forms: intentional and unintentional (clueless).** Some people use them deliberately as a "safer" form of racism, sexism, or homophobia, while others unknowingly perpetuate harm due to ignorance.

- **They are often dismissed as harmless or a sign of oversensitivity.** This makes it difficult for individuals to address them without being perceived as "too sensitive" or "difficult."

- **Microaggressions create a hostile work environment, even when unintentional.** They signal to the recipient that they don't fully belong, eroding confidence, productivity, and well-being.

- **Remain professional but respond with clarity and authority.** A direct, calm response sets boundaries, reinforces expectations, and shows that microaggressions won't be ignored.

- **Everyone should speak up against microaggressions.** If you witness a microaggression, don't leave it to the person targeted to respond. Speaking up for others sets a precedent that these behaviors will not be tolerated.

The Ups and Downs of the Ego-First Leader

"While at a dinner with the CEO and a few other execs, the CEO, my boss, asked me how my wife was doing. I told him she had recently injured herself and had been sick lately. He responded: 'Well, as long as she is still putting out.'"

—"Ted," interview with a former coworker

THROUGHOUT MY CAREER, I have worked for many leaders—VPs, CEOs, division heads—in large and small companies. I have worked for many engaged and empathetic leaders who strived to grow their organizations for the benefit of all stakeholders. I have also enjoyed great relationships with most of the leaders I've worked for.

Reflecting on some individuals who may have fallen short of that standard, some common personality traits—big ego, arrogance, controlling nature, incessant bragging, lack of empathy, and unethical behavior—emerged that I thought were worth investigating. To my surprise, there's an abundance of research, studies, and articles on what we can politely label "ego-first leaders."

And here's yet another unspoken element we have to deal with while navigating our careers: recognizing these toxic traits in others, understanding how they impact us, and figuring out how to respond without derailing our own progress. As with the other forms of bias and discrimination discussed in this book, identifying this issue is the first step in devising plans to address it.

Clive Boddy, an associate professor at Anglia Ruskin University in England, coined the term "corporate psychopaths" in an article he published in 2015. In that article, he defines corporate psychopaths as "those psychopaths who exist successfully in society and work within corporations. They are conceptualized as highly career-oriented but ruthless, unethical, and exploitative employees."[1]

There are several other studies about corporate psychopaths, which estimate that between 8 and 20 percent of all CEOs fall into this category.[2]

A related concept in leadership psychopathy is known as the Dark Triad, which outlines three traits that can afflict CEOs: narcissism, Machiavellianism, and psychopathy/sociopathy.[3]

A narcissist has an unreasonably high sense of importance; they need and seek attention and admiration. They display boundless arrogance and embody entitlement. Machiavellianism is more focused, a personality that seeks power through a calculated focus on self-interest. Those afflicted are indifferent to morality and lack empathy for others. Psychopaths who lack empathy can be callous, and that lack of empathy enables them to be highly manipulative. [4]

Despite their potential for charisma and creativity, research suggests that corporate psychopaths often harm organizations through unethical behavior, bullying, and creating hostile work environments.

Snakes in Suits, a book by Paul Babiak, PhD, and Robert D. Hare, PhD, is dedicated to this subject. The book explores the presence and impact of psychopathic individuals within the corporate world. It explains how these people infiltrate organizations, manipulate their way up the corporate ladder, and create toxic work environments. It explores the common psychological traits of corporate psychopaths, such as charm, manipulation, lack of empathy, and unethical behavior.

Some of this research has been disputed, and there are differing opinions about how many of these "corporate psychopaths" exist. I have worked for one CEO who clearly fit the description and another who was pretty close. The degree to which CEOs—whether male or female—display aberrant behaviors varies from mild and occasional to more consistently extreme.

Many examples I share in this chapter are my experiences with CEOs. However, it is important to note that a person doesn't suddenly become an ego-first leader after reaching the CEO level. These traits develop long before they attain this position. You will and probably are now encountering this personality type in your manager or vice president—I know I have. Throughout this chapter, we'll use the terms "CEO" and "ego-first leader" interchangeably.

Understanding the Ego-First Leader

Problematic behavior by leaders can be challenging and stress-inducing if you don't understand how to react, respond, or detach yourself to remain objective, professional—and happy—at work. In this chapter, we discuss how the bad behavior of an ego-first leader will manifest and how it may impact you. I share practical strategies to navigate these situations effectively to ensure you maintain well-being and happiness at work.

Let's start by exploring why so many of these personality types are attracted to the most senior leadership roles and how ego-first leadership shows up in the workplace.

Vision, Strategy, and Ability to Juggle Priorities

Successful CEOs have a clear vision and a compelling strategy. They understand their products and the needs of their customers. They know how to build an empowering and inclusive culture, hire the right people, and when to let go of those who are not a good fit for the job or the culture.

Senior leadership roles come with inherent pressures. They must build the vision and convince a large group of people—board members, shareholders, executive team, employees, customers, and partners—of their vision and that they are the right person for the job.

While trying to build a consistently profitable company, they juggle many priorities: technological advances, competitive threats, creating a culture that keeps employees motivated, and building and leading a team to implement the vision.

It's a lot of work and constant pressure, which requires someone who can thrive when surrounded by at least occasional chaos. An over-sized ego can be a genuine asset to someone in that position. They need to believe they can overcome all obstacles and convince investors and other stakeholders that they can build a successful company.

Confidence and False Empathy

A big ego and self-confidence can help people graduate to the execu-tive level and successfully maintain that position. I don't kid myself; my confidence and ego have also helped me become successful in my career. My peers and I discuss this often when faced with a leader with a big ego. Ego and confidence aren't problems, per se, but an outsized ego can be.

Leaders with oversized egos aren't easy to work for and can infringe on the company culture. Executives largely define the culture; they tend to surround themselves with others like them or expect those they hire to behave similarly or accept, promote, and admire that behavior. This can metastasize as toxicity within a company.

Narcissists require validation and recognition from others. This may manifest when they tell you what great things they did for you and the company. Bragging is common.

While they may lack empathy and care only about themselves, they do know how to fake compassion at the right times, and this can create confusion. I have witnessed leaders who would make bold claims of compassion in front of others with such things as sick leave, vacation time, or having to let someone go, but in private, they would show their lack of patience and compassion for such situations. In their minds, you are a disposable asset.

When my aunt passed away, and I came back to work one day after the funeral, the CEO commented to one of my peers that I needed to get over my grieving. I wasn't being "my cheerful self," which annoyed him.

These ego-first leaders have a great sense of entitlement. Their entitlement is rooted in the feeling that they deserve certain privileges over others. They may take credit for others' work because they have to be seen as the ones who thought of every great idea, strategy, or plan.

The biggest concern is when a CEO only feels comfortable surrounded by people they think they can be themselves around. They don't want to have to check their temper or moderate language or behavior. This is why many women get excluded from leadership positions. These types of CEOs don't want to worry about being reported or fired for bad behavior, so they prefer not to have women (or people of color) in the room.

Working for the Ego-First Leader

You may know a leader in your company who fits this description, or you may even be working with one now. Most of these ego-first leaders didn't start as CEOs, unless they founded the company. They were managers, directors, and vice presidents first. They emerged from the pool of people who are currently your peers or managers.

The people around you may become CEOs one day. As they rise through the ranks, you must learn to work with them and their behaviors—good and bad. We have explored how to manage your career through many of the most challenging situations you have or might experience, from sexism to racism to ageism to microaggressions. You will likewise have to learn to manage your career alongside ego-first leaders. You must learn how to work with them and be a productive employee within the culture they create.

I have worked for many CEOs and have had great relationships with most of them. That is not to say that it wasn't difficult at times. It can be even more challenging if you, too, have an ego. The following pages share some of my experiences and those of others who have worked for problematic leaders and provide strategies for successfully dealing with and working with similar leaders.

We must remember that it can be hard for these professionals to stay grounded when so many around them feed their sense of power and tell them that they are right more often than wrong.

The Control Freak

It can be challenging to work with ego-centric and controlling leaders. Although ego has fueled their success, it can also lead to tight controls and an inability to empower teams to do what they do best. I have seen CEOs get so involved in product development that they hinder the product management and engineering teams from following best practices, like researching what customers truly need. CEOs with big egos and strong personalities don't allow room for constructive feedback.

One CEO I worked with was controlling everything, down to the design of marketing materials. I don't mean the company logo or brand, which they should have a say in, nor do I mean when a CEO and I are working together to try to figure out how to message something or visualize a concept through design. I mean the CEO who insists on reviewing all data sheets and nitpicks the color of the subheadings in a paragraph. He did not limit his controlling nature to Marketing; he did this in all departments, and it was oppressive.

Over a short period, I witnessed the ramifications of such insistence on control. This CEO stifled progress. Executives and their teams were afraid to make decisions without his approval. No one felt empowered. It was like a bunch of children seeking their teacher's permission to do everything. It was a toxic culture. The employees were not happy; they often felt humiliated and undervalued. The company was not successful. How could it be? If someone is that involved in the minutiae, how could he possibly do his job as a CEO? And in these situations, the talented people leave.

This controlling CEO demanded that everyone follow his way of doing things and his interests—like sports or his political affiliation. He was elitist and entitled. He viewed his executive staff as a reflection of himself. He wanted us to emulate him.

He did not like the car that one of the executives drove. This executive had a few children attending college and couldn't afford a new car. The CEO pressured him into buying a nicer car that he could not afford, which caused him to worry about the loan he had to take out to purchase the vehicle.

The CEO and I had a meeting in another building on campus. I offered to drive us. We got in my car, and he was excited. "Wow! Look at you driving this fancy car," he said. He was thrilled. I had scored points just because my car met his requirements.

Entitled and Unethical

One of the characteristics of corporate psychopaths is that they can exhibit bad behavior. This CEO certainly did. It was rooted in his sense of entitlement. This CEO saw the company as his personal playground, bending the rules whenever it suited him. If he wanted something, company funds covered it—no questions asked. Lavish perks, personal indulgences disguised as business expenses, and blatant favoritism were all part of the culture he created.

One particular situation stood out. A significant expense showed up in my department's budget, and when I questioned it, the CFO reluctantly admitted what had happened. The CEO had orchestrated an elaborate outing for himself and his inner circle, passing it off as a corporate event. The CFO had been pulled into it as well, clearly uneasy about the entire thing.

Over time, I had several conversations with the CFO, who confided in me about the growing pressure to approve questionable expenditures. He knew the risks but felt trapped. I warned him that, as CFO, he would be held just as accountable as the CEO if things went south. We talked about well-known corporate scandals where financial leaders had taken the fall. Eventually, as the company's financial health declined, he made the difficult choice to leave.

Beyond financial misman-agement, the CEO blurred the lines between personal and com-pany resources in other ways. Employees were expected to take on personal tasks for him, often during work hours. Business funds were used to finance projects that had nothing to do with the com-pany. Even holiday celebrations were leveraged for his benefit, with company money covering expenses that seemed to serve only his personal interests.

Despite the company strug-gling, the CEO insisted on hosting an executive retreat—against the advice of many on the leadership team. Concerns were raised about how it would look to employees, but he dismissed them.

> If the CEO wanted something, company funds covered it— no questions asked. Lavish perks, personal indulgences disguised as business expenses, and blatant favoritism were all part of the culture he created.

The retreat was held at an upscale venue, complete with high-end gifts for the executives—premium gear, personalized items, the kind of things that felt tone-deaf given the company's financial strug-gles. Sure enough, word got out. Employees were furious. To them, it looked like leadership was indulging itself while asking everyone else to do more with less. It was a terrible message, and many of us knew it.

But the CEO? He didn't care. The backlash didn't faze him in the slightest.

Pushing Opinions on Others

One year, his party lost a presidential election, but that did not stop him from talking about politics. In fact, it fueled his discussions. In staff meetings, he would criticize the new president and his party. He would tell us all the reasons why his party should have won, or if something came up in the news, he would give his opinion with a strong political slant. It was inappropriate conversation for the workplace. The executive staff would sit there and not say a word. It was uncomfortable for everyone. Even those who agreed with his politics felt uncomfortable. But he didn't care. The more we didn't react, the more he preached.

It was the same for sports. He was a sports fanatic. He would talk about sports in staff meetings and make fun of those who didn't watch the game or didn't like or understand sports. He was a bully. He forced sporting events at work, including softball and volleyball, insisting everyone participate.

He was fit. He asked me if I worked out in the morning. "Yes, I do—usually around five thirty," I responded. "See! Kae works out in the morning too," he would say to my peers to humiliate those who did not work out.

His disdain for people who were not fit and certainly for those who were overweight was palpable. He talked nonstop about the weight of some of the employees. He created fitness contests at work and gave the executive staff gifts focused on fitness.

Indeed, there is nothing wrong with promoting a healthy lifestyle at work, but he forced it on people and bullied those not interested in fitness. He thought everyone should be like him. One employee told me that a few of her teammates feared being fired because they were overweight. Imagine having that stress at work. This is the same CEO who told the CFO to let me know that he preferred my hair out after I wore it in a ponytail for a presentation.

Dealing with these Behaviors

Not all executives or CEOs will exhibit such extreme behavior. Still, I have worked with many CEOs who demonstrate some of these behaviors—bragging, arrogance, nobody knows more than they do, always being right, and not taking or considering anyone's feedback well. You can't dispute them, certainly not in front of others, and they immediately dismiss you if you do.

In these situations, my strategy is to discuss things privately with them. By gradually building my rapport and credibility with them, I can eventually provide an opinion in front of others without the leader feeling that they are being challenged. Building credibility with your peers is also crucial—if your leader sees that your peers value your input, they will be less inclined to feel slighted in meetings if you offer suggestions. It is all in how you approach the conversation; a calm, nonconfrontational approach tends to work best.

As a woman, I have sensed the different treatment from male CEOs and other leaders. They interact with me differently than they do with men. They speak to me differently; they feel they are being more respectful by not berating me or using profanity with or in front of me, but there is a downside. It means they consider me differently than the men. They aren't as comfortable around me as they are with the men. We spoke about this in Chapter 3, dealing with sexism. Women in the workplace—especially in tech—are left out of certain situations because of this discomfort.

We were recording a corporate video to use in our marketing programs. I wanted the CEO in the video to show our thought leadership. I wrote the script for the CEO and set up a video team to come in and tape his part of the video. I was in the room—as I had been with others who would be in the video. I had reviewed the script with the others. I coached them through sections where they were struggling, offering suggestions for better ways to say things or giving general support. I had worked with two other people before the CEO came in. They seemed to appreciate that I was there helping them.

The CEO, who had a big ego, as I'd witnessed on several occasions, came into the room, and we started. He stumbled a few times. We would stop, and I would give him words of encouragement. He kept struggling, which isn't unusual when doing videos; everybody struggles a bit. He stopped and said he wanted a break. We took a break, and my boss, the CMO (I was the Marketing VP), called me into his office and told me that the CEO didn't want me in the room while he recorded his part. He said I made him uncomfortable, and he wanted the CMO in the room instead. Mind you, the CMO had not been involved with the video project, so I had to quickly get him up to speed on what we were trying to accomplish and the CEO's part. I will add that I was the only female in the company other than the receptionist. Perhaps this CEO did not want to look foolish in front of a woman.

Men Who Surround Themselves with Other Men

Some male leaders prefer to be surrounded by other men so they don't have to adjust what they say and how they behave. If you are in high tech, you understand the fast pace and the everyday pressures to innovate while keeping the competition at bay. For the CEO, that pressure is exponentially greater. They want to lead their team without the hassle of caring about what they say or how they say it. They want to move fast. If they have to hesitate and hide their behavior from certain people on their team—such as women or other minorities—it's easier not to have them on the team or in the room.

While there are ego-first female leaders—think Elizabeth Holmes, the founder of Theranos who was convicted of fraud for misleading investors and patients about her company's blood-testing technology—most CEOs in the US tech industry are men, and they dictate the culture. Men usually feel more comfortable around other men. They can speak to men differently than they can speak to women; they do not have to be as careful around men in what they say, how they behave, and how they treat others. As our culture has become more sensitive to sexism, racism, and other forms of discrimination, these CEOs don't want to worry about what they say at work—so they hire people like them. This is how toxic, homogenous cultures get created and propagated.

In my research for this book, I approached several male professional contacts inquiring as to what they could offer about the ego-first leader. One respondent, whom I will call "Derek," told me he'd worked for a handful of tech CEOs over the years. He witnessed a number of issues.

> Some [CEOs] have learned—the hard way—that when they let their guard down, when they cut loose, some things they say or do can be an unintended source of discomfort or subsequent complaint. They have tried to curtail that behavior, to avoid that

liability, but it is—somehow—essential to who they are. They can't "be themselves" without being "that way."

Military and sports metaphors are frequently used to frame solutions to business challenges (product/market fit, expense management, client retention) rooted in the unity of the leadership team. A minority of the men (and they were all men) under whom I've worked were convinced that the key to getting the team to think and act as one was best accomplished through bonding events. This leads to off-hours meetups, off-site sessions, and (after too much Barolo) off-colored comments.

Much consideration was given to making additions or changes to the leadership team, lest the new person "wasn't a good fit culturally." Are we going to be able to continue to "be us" with this change? This mindset makes adding women/gay/trans to the management mix a real risk. Even the "cool ones"—likely to ignore aberrant behavior—could still take notes, complain to investors, or otherwise go public. Liability in waiting—and one that is easily avoided by keeping anyone who wasn't willing to "play ball" out of the room.

The temptation to keep [the HR department] a lower-level function, or severely restrict its executive presence, ensures there is no "thought police" to curtail the boys from being boys.

Some of the things I've heard from senior executives?

"Well, at least we don't have to look at that fat, ugly bitch anymore."

"He's dumb as a day-old nigger."

"We need to put a bullet in that whole department."[5]

Even without any of the behind-the-scenes details, this exclusion wears on you, especially when you have worked hard at mastering your craft, advancing your career, earning years of experience, and knowing full well you are qualified in your profession. You will have to navigate these personalities now and as you build your career.

Assessing Where You Stand

Aside from your financial situation, one of the decision points when working for someone who exhibits these behaviors is how much this person controls how you work. What is the degree to which they control your area of the business or your decisions? Are you able to make most decisions? Is this person reasonable? Can you build a rapport with them and earn credibility enough to persuade them to hear your views on impactful decisions, or are you merely implementing what they tell you to do?

You could be at risk if the only thing you can execute is what this ego-first CEO wants.

Here's why: If a CEO or boss is so controlling and dictates what you and your team do, they will eventually come to believe they must always tell you what to do because you can't think "on your own." I have experienced this kind of gaslighting. Because of their ego and inability to find fault in themselves, they will never admit they have created this dynamic by controlling every decision. I watch this closely when I am up against a leader who is not collaborative.

I will do what they ask, still do my job, and run my department as I know how. I share my views on things I disagree with if they are important to the business. I also express when I agree with something; or if there is something that they have done well for the employees or business, I give them that recognition. We all need positive reinforcement. Validation is key. Senior leaders need validation, too, and the ego-first leader needs more validation than others. Showing your value to your leader is also key.

Don't Ask for Their Opinions

What I don't do is fall into the trap of asking their opinion on everything. I saw the ramifications of this with the highly controlling CEO I described previously. The whole company stalled; they could not make decisions without him getting involved. It delays everything, it is not good for business, and it can sneak up on you if you are not paying attention. As you build your relationship with your leader and collaborate on various tasks and projects, you can easily fall into the trap of asking their opinion on things they should not be spending time on.

This is especially true if they have a strong personality and strong opinions on everything. Throughout your collaboration, you may start to understand their hot buttons and may be reluctant to make decisions in those areas without checking with them first. You can even unknowingly pass this reluctance on to your team. This happened to me.

One time my team was working on a piece of content, and they asked if we should run it by the CEO first to get his feedback. I almost said yes because I knew he had strong opinions on how we messaged things. But I stopped myself. I said, "No, let's go with it. You were trained on the new messaging; we understand how to target an audience."

Having worked for a variety of leaders over the years, and having my own track record of successes and failures in my work, I am comfortable making mistakes or having something fail. I can deal with the results and repercussions. I was hired for a reason, which isn't to have the CEO tell me everything I need to do to run my department. He ultimately doesn't want that, nor should he be doing it. If he does, it's not a good fit for either of us.

But I'll admit that it took me a while to feel comfortable with this concept.

As I have said, I have seen controlling and arrogant behavior stifle an organization. Nothing good comes of it. The CEO or senior leader can burn out or become unfocused on their job if they are laser-focused on everyone else's. That is a lose-lose situation, and you should start looking for another job where your skills and experience are valued.

This is not to say that your leader is controlling if they tell you to do something, even if you disagree. Sometimes, they have a clear vision of where the company needs to go, and what they ask you to do is an important element of that strategy. You know the difference. You know when it's occasional or critical versus controlling, ego-centered, and simply arrogant.

Build a Productive Relationship with the Ego-First Leader

Navigating difficult relationships can be trying at times and requires you to put your ego aside frequently. Here are a few strategies for building a great working relationship with an ego-first leader.[6]

Recognize Who They Are

Recognize that they are someone with a big ego. Having this awareness goes a long way when dealing with their behavior. When they are arrogant, they need to be right or be able to brag. Separating yourself from this—knowing it is not about you—can make this easier. As long as it is harmless bragging, and not taking away from team dynamics or morale by overlooking their contributions, let it happen and sometimes validate their ego. It lets them know you are on their side and are there to support their efforts.

Help Them Succeed

Recognize the enormity of their role and the pressure they receive. Let them know that you understand this. Help and support them by doing a great job in your area and being a team player. Don't cause them friction.

Be a leader in your group. Make suggestions for improvements that will help the team or company succeed. As an example, two people had recently left our company, and I knew we had a company meeting coming up. I suggested we have the meeting sooner and share our progress to get the employees excited about our future.

Show Your Value

You must constantly show value to your leader. Be proactive on projects, processes, and policies that drive your department or the company forward. Remember that in the mind of the ego-first leader, people are disposable. If you are not valuable to them, you can be replaced. Showing value to them includes showing value to the rest of your team or the organization. Again, be a leader.

Maintain Boundaries

You will have to create boundaries with this leader. You can verbalize boundaries by letting them know your workload, role and responsibilities, and personal space. Or you can simply not engage when you witness behaviors you disagree with—such as speaking badly about one of your peers or shaming someone in a public forum. When they do this, they typically seek a reaction from others. Don't react.

Correct Any Misinformation

You may find that your leader makes outlandish statements. They may tend to overstate something—good or bad. It can be as simple as "The sales team has no tools from Marketing" or as damaging as "The Marketing programs aren't producing any pipeline." You must correct these statements firmly and at every turn. You must have a good sense of timing because sometimes it will be essential to correct the misinformation when it is stated, which may be in front of other people. Other times, it may make sense to correct the misinformation one-on-one.

Developing a good understanding of timing requires observation in meetings. See how your leader reacts when someone else corrects them. If they don't respond well, you may want to correct the information privately or wait until you have built a strong rapport with them.

Remember, egotists will consider any correction a challenge to their authority, so think twice before doing it in front of others. If they respond by challenging you, consider dropping it and returning to it later when you are alone with them. "Hey, I wanted to circle back on what you said about Marketing's contribution to the pipeline." Share with them why it is vital to get this correct—such as showing them the numbers and letting them know it's important to the health of the Sales and Marketing relationship and the morale of the marketing team to acknowledge that Marketing is creating a pipeline for the company. Be specific. "In fact, we are creating 25 percent of all new opportunities . . ."

With Experience Comes Wisdom

As you navigate the complexities of working with ego-first leaders, you're not just learning how to cope with challenging personalities but you're also developing a deeper awareness of your leadership style. This awareness will shape the kind of leader you aspire to be and the culture you can help create.

I've been fortunate to work with some truly exceptional leaders throughout my career. They were collaborative, respectful, and transparent. They valued my expertise and led with kindness rather than provoked turmoil. These leaders created environments where I could thrive, and their approach to leadership inspired me to do the same for others. They proved that success doesn't require the negative traits of an ego-first leader; true leadership fosters trust, empowers teams, and cultivates a positive culture.

The traits that help ego-driven leaders succeed in high-pressure roles—confidence, decisiveness, and resilience—can be powerful when balanced with humility and empathy. By observing good and challenging leaders, you will develop a framework for the type of leader you want to become. You also have the opportunity to break the cycle, demonstrating that leadership driven by respect and collaboration can achieve remarkable success.

Ego-first leaders can be challenging, but as we've explored, there are strategies for successfully navigating these relationships. As with every challenge raised in this book, understanding your choices and options empowers you to build your career on your terms, even in the face of obstacles. These trials often make us stronger.

In the final chapter, I share the fundamental principles I've honed over the years to become a successful female leader in a male-dominated industry. My journey hasn't always been easy, but each experience has shaped the leader I am today—and I hope it inspires you to shape your path with courage and confidence. The more we showcase how a great leader should behave and still achieve success, the more we can redefine what true leadership looks like and create cultures where everyone can thrive.

CLOSING THOUGHTS

Working with ego-first leaders can be challenging, but by understanding their behavior, recognizing their need for validation, and setting boundaries, you can manage the relationship while also growing as a leader and shaping your own leadership style.

- **Ego-first leaders are often charismatic.** But they also cause significant harm through unethical behavior, lack of empathy, and the creation of hostile work environments.

- **These traits don't develop overnight.** Ego-first behavior tends to emerge long before someone becomes a CEO, and you may encounter such personalities even at the managerial level.

- **Ego-first leaders thrive on validation.** Recognizing their achievements can help you maintain a more positive relationship with them.

Where Do You Go from Here?

"I raise up my voice—not so I can shout, but so that those without a voice
can be heard . . . We cannot succeed when half of us are held back."

—Malala Yousafzai, 16th Birthday Speech at the United Nations

I WAS EATING DINNER at my favorite restaurant when I recognized someone seated at a nearby table. "That's Bob!" I exclaimed to my husband. I approached the table and said, "Hi, Bob."

"Kae! Oh, my goodness. Wow."

Bob was a former colleague from many moons ago. We reminisced for a bit, catching up on who we are still in touch with at the old company, and talked about what a great place that company was to work for, how young we were back then, and how "old" we were now. We parted with an invite from Bob and his wife to dine at their house soon. It was amazing to see Bob again.

The next night, my husband and I were at dinner in another part of Massachusetts, enjoying a summer evening meal on the restaurant's patio. We heard someone call out to us, and lo and behold, there was another person we had worked with. We joked for a few minutes, and then, after dinner, he joined us on the patio for drinks and dessert. We caught up on life, kids, and work.

I cherish moments like these, seeing kind, intelligent people I have shared some experiences with and can pick up as if there weren't a decade (or two) in between. These moments remind me that beyond the challenges we face in our careers, there is a deeper joy in the lasting relationships we create and the experiences we share.

My Amazing Journey

This book covers some heavy subject matter and explores challenging experiences I and others have had and will continue to endure. While exploring these challenges is essential, I want to acknowledge the possibility and meaning your career can afford you. The point of this book isn't to help you survive corporate life. It's to help you have an impactful, joyful career you love and to also lead a beautiful life while building it.

I live an amazing life. Thanks to my job, I have traveled to many parts of the world and have friends in many places. I've gone whitewater rafting down a river in Bali, partied 'til the wee hours of the morning in Barcelona, and drank at a speakeasy in Cannes. I've shopped in London and Paris, attended Octoberfest in Munich, toured around Singapore and Sydney, and hung out at many beer gardens in Vienna—all with wonderful coworkers.

I've worked with many people from different cultures, which has given me a greater appreciation for cultural differences. I met my husband at work. I found a profession that I love, and I feel pride in my proficiency. I have had the pleasure of helping companies grow and have led fantastic marketing teams—large and small. I have learned a lot about people and how to appreciate and work with many personalities. I have learned to lead. Due to my professional experience, I am a much better communicator and collaborator.

My career has helped me smooth out parts of my personality that needed it and helped me become more confident and less fearful. I learned how vital respect is—giving and commanding it—for myself. I learned how and when to speak up confidently, a skill set I lacked when I began this corporate journey. Through this career, I have gained the experience and wisdom to mentor others.

> The point of this book isn't to help you survive corporate life. It's to help you have an impactful, joyful career you love and to also lead a beautiful life while building it.

Helping people develop their careers and supporting them through situations explored in this book are things that bring me great satisfaction. I want to see more women and marginalized people succeed and have the opportunity to live the lives they want.

Parting Words of Advice

I have a strong support system of people from many regions of this world that I can reach out to for advice, to celebrate, or to gripe. And I want that for all of you. We all deserve to live our best lives, succeed at whatever we set out to do, and have a blast while doing it.

I have learned to navigate difficult work experiences by developing specific strategies and guiding principles that have shepherded my career. These principles were shaped through work experiences, experimentation with techniques to keep me moving forward, and values instilled in me from an early age. You can use these strategies in your current role and as you progress in your career.

Keep Improving

My dad told my sisters and me at a very young age that because we were women of color, we would have to work twice as hard as any man. I'm sure many of you got that same advice. It really stuck with me and created the work ethic I maintain today, my unwavering efforts to master my profession, and my determination to consistently deliver results.

The tech industry evolves quickly and will only get faster. You must keep up with the industry at large and the practice of your profession within that industry. Marketing has evolved greatly since I started my career. The martech stack, data analytics, marketing approaches, and principles continue to evolve. Whatever your profession is—product management, sales, customer success, or engineering—you must commit to continual education.

I've encountered people who don't think about their career development, and I don't mean getting promoted; I mean continuing to develop their professional skills. They come to work and take the same approach they always have. This may work for a while, but there are plenty of scenarios where this shortcoming becomes apparent: You have to look for another job, and that organization is utilizing the latest practices; your company gets acquired or merges, and there are people in the new company who have greater skills than you; or you get a new manager, and they recognize you are doing things the "old way."

When B2B marketing shifted from brand marketing to revenue marketing, which meant we were tied to a number similar to Sales, I witnessed many marketers rebel against this, and their careers stalled. A colleague of mine refused to embrace the change and stuck to her typical approach to marketing, delivering campaigns with no thought to business results—ROI and revenue. I watched her continue to lose roles as a result.

Deliver Value

You can't skate through your career and expect to go far. You must keep up with your profession and industry: read articles, attend conferences and webinars, and talk to others in your profession and industry. Look at it as part of your job—because it is. You are paid to be the best at your job, to evolve your role or department, and to deliver maximum value to the company every single day.

I focus on delivering value—implementing processes and executing programs that help me achieve the goals set out for me and help the company achieve its goals. Many people I have worked with meander through the workweek without accomplishing anything meaningful. Don't think this goes unnoticed. To succeed in your role, you must stay diligent and deliver value.

Align Your Job with Your Goals

Throughout this book, we've explored challenges that can derail careers, such as Nicki in Chapter 6 on racism, who experienced a group of people intent on making it clear that she didn't belong because she wasn't White, or Kristine in Chapter 4 on sexual harassment, who lost her job for speaking up against her CEO and also had a job rescinded when she asked about the company's sexual harassment policies, making her a legal liability. Despite these setbacks, Nicki and Kristine stayed focused on their goals. They refused to settle for any job; they searched until they found jobs aligned with their career aspirations.

I also take this approach in my career. I weigh every opportunity in terms of my ultimate vision: Will it provide me with a critical skill, such as functional leadership or global experience? Will it allow me to manage larger teams or gain expertise in a new aspect of my profession, like artificial intelligence? Having a clear vision makes it easier to pursue opportunities for growth.

Some situations, especially when your safety and mental health are at risk, may compel you to leave your current role. However, think through your decision to depart. It may provide some near-term empowerment (I showed them!), but a snap decision could set you back financially or developmentally. Always weigh the short-term relief against the long-term impact on your goals.

I have built my career by embracing opportunities as they unfolded, even if the path wasn't linear. I've started businesses, led divisions, taken roles without experience, and even accepted a demotion to gain expertise that ultimately advanced my career. Taking risks is crucial. If it doesn't work out—after a solid effort—then course correct and keep moving. The key is to have a clear end game. Define your vision, craft a plan, and be willing to adapt.

Stand Up for Yourself and Others

You are the CEO of your career. Stay focused on your goals and take charge of your journey. Don't let someone else's ignorance or actions derail you. Stand up against sexism, harassment, racism, ageism, and the other biases that might try to hold you—or those around you—down. Use the strategies from each chapter to maneuver through or around them and move on. Stay focused.

I have had many people—bosses, peers, and other influential people—support me, help me develop, and offer opportunities, but I never relied solely on them. I own the success of my career. I don't wait for others to create my opportunities, nor do I let external challenges dictate my path.

You will likely encounter many of the situations we discuss in this book. Navigating these situations requires mastering skills like conflict resolution, reading a room, and effective communication. I am sure you know this, but knowing isn't enough—you must actively practice them, even when it's hard. And it will be hard at times. What will set you apart as a professional is mastering them. Remember,

> You are the CEO of your career. Stay focused on your goals and take charge of your journey. Don't let someone else's ignorance or actions derail you. Stand up against sexism, harassment, racism, ageism, and the other biases that might try to hold you—or those around you—down.

your goal is to succeed in your career and achieve the vision you have set for yourself.

Remain Calm and Professional

We all know conflicts are inevitable. Can you step back and view the situation objectively to understand the other person's perspective? Can you let go of your ego and the pain of past experiences and remain calm, even in the face of bias and unfairness? I won't pretend it's easy—I work on it continuously. Staying composed and professional, even when emotions are high, helps to resolve conflicts more effectively and professionally. Composure defies the biases that may already exist about you.

Read the Room

The ability to read a room sounds easy enough, but it requires constant attention. Think back to meetings you've attended. Who has the real influence? Who sets the tone? Who commands respect? Who is likely to derail the conversation? I've seen careers take hits because someone didn't grasp the dynamics in the room. Like the new salesperson who joked about the CEO, thinking it was okay to be so familiar with him in front of others. The joke didn't land well. Or the colleague who jabs at a peer to make herself look better but comes off as petty and unprofessional.

Situational awareness is critical to your success. Remain observant of reactions and verbal and nonverbal cues and adjust your approach accordingly. This is about empathy and a high EQ—emotional quotient. Mastering this will help you avoid missteps and effectively navigate meetings.

Be a Good Communicator

Communication ties all of this together. Being a great communicator isn't just about talking; it's about listening—really listening. As they say, you don't learn while talking; you learn while listening. How often do you rush to speak without letting someone else finish what they are trying to convey?

Listening first allows for better responses and fewer misunderstandings. It isn't easy, as we all want to get our points across. Becoming a great listener takes time. It did for me, anyway. I am a decent communicator, clear and direct, but being a great listener takes time and practice. It is also about being respectful of others. Assume that what they have to say is essential to hear. Understand that they took the time to communicate something for a reason, something that is important to them. Give them the floor and let them speak.

Let's not underestimate the power of clear and concise communication, especially in the situations we have discussed. It is a critical skill. Be direct and transparent about your message and expectations. Effective communication demands confidence—the confidence in accepting that your words may not be well received or may be disputed, yet you speak with clarity and purpose anyway. Don't let that deter you. Conversations approached with precision and confidence will resolve faster and more effectively.

Nurture a Strong Support System at Work

I couldn't have achieved success in my career—or handled the challenges of bias, discrimination, and brutal workplace cultures—without solid support systems both inside and outside of work. They've made all the difference.

Let's face it: We're working in a system built by men, for men. This system was not made for you. Because of this, you will continue to face bias and discrimination. The goal is to find solutions that help you challenge that bias, claim your space, and thrive in a system that wasn't designed with you in mind. One of the most powerful tools for doing so is to nurture a strong support system at work—people who believe in your potential, advocate for you, and offer guidance when the challenges feel overwhelming. With the right support, you can navigate these barriers and not just survive but truly thrive. It is possible to build a career that brings you success, satisfaction, and joy.

Remember when I shared my story about experiencing sexual harassment? At the time, I didn't tell anyone. I went through it alone, and that took a severe emotional toll. If I'd had a support system to lean on, I could have alleviated some of that stress. Having a safe space to share what I was going through would have been incredibly helpful.

Now, I rely heavily on my support networks at work and beyond. Building solid relationships inside an organization is vital. When I start at a new company, I immediately focus on internal networking. Success isn't a solo journey. Greatness happens when you collaborate with others. I've seen people fail because they tried to do everything alone. A good leader doesn't work in isolation. They seek different viewpoints, which helps create better plans and decisions.

Connecting with people at all levels of the company is essential, not just those on your immediate team. Reach out to people who can add value—maybe they have deep product knowledge or a quick tip about using a spreadsheet. I've found that these connections help me achieve goals faster and make collaboration smoother. Plus, let's face it: Having friends at work makes the day-to-day so much better.

These internal networks become even more crucial as you advance in your career. Sometimes you need advice on things you can't discuss with your team. Having trusted colleagues you can turn to makes a huge difference.

And there's another benefit: Building internal relationships helps break down biases. My mother once said that people who live near each other understand each other's struggles. The same is true at work. When you collaborate and build relationships, you allow others to see your true value. Over time, this earns you respect and credibility and can chip away at biases.

Strengthen Your External Support System

Your external support system—outside work—is just as important as the one in the office. I have a colleague who's a CMO at a tech firm, and we meet regularly to talk about marketing and leadership. Recently, she needed to vent about frustrating meetings with her new CEO. Even though her team delivered 90 percent of the company's pipeline, he questioned her work, and she started doubting herself. We discussed it, and I reminded her of her expertise and success. By the end of the call, she felt more confident. Sometimes we need someone outside our workplace to remind us of our worth, especially when self-doubt creeps in.

This support is even more critical when dealing with bias or discrimination. Many people instantly question their own experiences. "Did that really happen?" they wonder. Having a support system helps you process those tough questions. Should you speak up? Are you being too sensitive? How will it affect your career? These are challenging situations to navigate alone. Talking them through with someone you trust can be life-changing.

Beyond emotional support, your external network can also help professionally. Over the years, I've built a network of people I trust for advice, brainstorming, and learning new skills. These connections have become invaluable—not just for emotional support but also for career opportunities.

The key to networking is to give as much as you get. Build real relationships. Be there for others when they need support, and they'll be there for you. Networking isn't about asking for help when you need a job. It's about creating a community that you can rely on—and that can depend on you.

Building strong relationships through networking creates a support system that can guide you through tough decisions, including one of the hardest: knowing when it's time to walk away.

Know When to Quit

Walking away isn't easy, but sometimes it's the right move. I've worked for companies where I loved the people, the technology, and the role. But not every company is like that. If you're in a place where the culture doesn't align with your values, you're not advancing, or the environment is just toxic, you must consider your options.

I remember working for a company where I was the only female executive—not unusual for me—but this time, it felt different. It was a good ol' boys' club. I wasn't valued or heard, and I was miserable. I spent almost a year trying to change things and speaking up about my frustrations, but nothing worked. Eventually, I realized I couldn't succeed there and couldn't help my team succeed either. So, I left.

Deciding to walk away is tough, and it's not a decision you make lightly. Talk to your support system. Look at your financial situation. Weigh the pros and cons carefully. It doesn't mean you should leave every time difficulties arise. If you find yourself hopping from job to job, it's worth reflecting: Is it really the environment, or is there something you need to address within yourself? Maybe it's fear of failure or difficulty with feedback. Whatever it is, find ways to cope—whether through meditation, exercise, therapy, or something else that works for you.

> We can't afford to take anything for granted, because this system wasn't built for us. Our joy and success matter too much to assume anything or to remain quiet when we encounter bias and discrimination.

Give Voice to Unspoken Issues

But walking away is just one part of the equation. Speaking up is the other, and it's at the heart of this book. So much of what we face in the workplace is tacitly accepted and goes unaddressed. But staying silent only perpetuates the cycle. You need to advocate for yourself and others. When you see bad behavior, call it out. When you experience it, voice your concerns. Speaking up doesn't just protect you—it sets a standard for how you expect to be treated and lets others know what's acceptable.

I get it—it's hard to speak up, especially when you're the one being targeted. Sometimes, we're too stunned, afraid, or worn down to advocate for ourselves. That's why it's extra powerful when others step in. Knowing someone has your back can make all the difference. And let me tell you that when perpetrators know people will speak up, they tend to think twice. We need to create environments where certain behaviors are simply unacceptable and everyone knows it.

Let's Lift Each Other Up

We have to build a community where we support each other and speak up not just for ourselves but for one another. It's about lifting each other up so we can create real change. I wrote this book because I stayed silent for too long and realized that by doing so, I wasn't helping the women around me or those who would come after me.

I'm at a stage in my career where I can reflect on both the journey I've taken and what still lies ahead. I couldn't step away from this profession I love without striving to make it better for you. My hope is that you can build a career that gives you the life you want, free from unnecessary doubt, frustration, or fear. We all deserve workplaces that are not just physically safe but emotionally safe too—places where we can show up as our whole, authentic selves without hesitation.

We have the right to thrive—just like anyone else—no matter our sex, race, beliefs, age, or experience. Others may take that privilege for granted because they're operating in a system made for them. We can't afford to take anything for granted, because this system wasn't built for us. Our joy and success matter too much to assume anything or to remain quiet when we encounter bias and discrimination. So, let's continue to speak up and be bold. Let's claim our space and help the women around us claim theirs too. When one of us raises our voice, others join in. That's how change happens.

Acknowledgments

THIS BOOK HAS BEEN a long time coming.

Many women generously shared their stories with me, often revisiting painful, frustrating, and at times demoralizing experiences. I won't name names in the interest of privacy, but you know who you are. My gratitude and admiration for your openness are endless. Thank you for the gift you gave me—and all the women who read this book. Your brave contributions validated the practical solutions in these pages. Any reader—especially women—has you to thank.

One fateful day in February 2024, I came across a LinkedIn post introducing me to Stacy Ennis, a book coach. I had no way of knowing then what profound impact reaching out to her would have on this journey. While my husband, Steve, encouraged me to write this book, Stacy showed me how to do it—and kept me on track every step of the way. She and her team wrapped their arms around me throughout the process, and I always felt fully supported. Stacy, I could not have written this without you. I'm so happy we met and thrilled that we've also built a friendship. You are such a warm and wonderful person—thank you!

Thank you to Greenleaf for your support in publishing this book and for introducing me to the editors who helped bring it to life: Elizabeth Brown, Maxine Marshall, and Jeanette Smith. A special thanks to Liz for helping shape the content and ensuring the themes and messages are clear and impactful for readers.

I'm also deeply grateful to the many family members, friends, and colleagues I talked with throughout the development of this book—who let me process ideas out loud, challenged and encouraged me, and helped clarify what I wanted to say. Kiersten, Kate, Victoria, Alex, Angela, and Delaney, thank you for those discussions, pre-read, and fantastic feedback. You improved the book by miles.

I am grateful to my parents, who believed women were as capable as men and raised their daughters accordingly. They exposed me to the world of books and language and brought me a lifetime of joy in reading and writing. They taught me the importance of continued education, speaking up for myself, and giving back to others. My whole heart wishes you were here to read this. I know a lively discussion would have ensued, enabling me to thank you for everything you gave me.

Lastly, thank you to Steve, my husband. Thank you for always being in my corner, supporting me throughout my career, and cheering me on through new endeavors like becoming an author.

Notes

Chapter 1

1. Susan J. Fowler, "Reflecting on One Very, Very Strange Year at Uber," February 19, 2017, https://www.susanjfowler.com/blog/2017/2/19/reflecting-on-one-very-strange -year-at-uber/.

2. Susan J. Fowler, "I Spoke Out Against Sexual Harassment at Uber. The Aftermath was more Terrifying than Anything I Faced Before," February 17, 2000, https://time.com /5784464/susan-fowler-book-uber-sexual-harassment/.

3. Nick Bilton, "The Chilling Reason Behind Travis Kalanick's Abrupt Resignation from Uber," *Vanity Fair*, June 21, 2017, https://www.vanityfair.com/news/2017/06/travis -kalanick-resignation-from-uber; Sarah Buhr, "Uber Delivers Letter of Sexual Harassment Probe Recommendations," *TechCrunch*, June 13, 2017, https://techcrunch .com/2017/06/13/uber-drops-sexual-harassment-probe-recommendations/.

4. "The State of Women in Tech and Startups 2023," Women Who Tech, accessed March 9, 2024, https://womenwhotech.org/data-and-resources/state-women-tech-and -startups-2023/.

5. "The State of Workplace Harassment 2021," AllVoices, September 1, 2021, https ://www.allvoices.co/blog/the-state-of-workplace-harassment-2021/.

6. William H. Frey, "The US Will Become 'Minority White' in 2045, Census Projects," Brookings, March 14, 2018, https://www.brookings.edu/articles/the-us-will-become -minority-white-in-2045-census-projects/.

7. Marie Bussing-Burks, "Women and Post-WWII Wages," *The Digest*, National Bureau of Economic Research, November 1, 2002, https://www.nber.org/digest/nov02/women -and-post-wwii-wages/.

8. Mitra Toossi, "A Century of Change: The U.S. Labor Force, 1950–2050," *Monthly Labor Review*, May 2002, https://www.bls.gov/opub/mlr/2002/05/art2full.pdf/.

9. US Bureau of Labor Statistics, "Labor Force Participation Rate—Women (LNS11300002)," Federal Reserve Economic Data (FRED), Federal Reserve Bank of St. Louis, accessed March 31, 2024, https://fred.stlouisfed.org/series/LNS11300002/.

10. US Equal Employment Opportunity Commission, "High Tech, Low Inclusion: Diversity in the High Tech Workforce and Sector, 2014–2022," September 2024, https://www.eeoc.gov/sites/default/files/2024-09/20240910_Diversity%20in%20the%20High%20Tech%20Workforce%20and%20Sector%202014-2022.pdf.

11. Maria Webb, "60+ Women in Tech Statistics You Need to Know in 2025: Trends, Gaps, and Challenges," Techopedia, updated March 25, 2024, https://www.techopedia.com/women-in-tech-statistics/.

12. "History of Women in the Workforce," Red Kap, July 9, 2020, https://www.redkap.com/women-workforce-history.html; US Equal Employment Opportunity Commission, "High Tech, Low Inclusion," https://www.eeoc.gov/sites/default/files/2024-09/20240910_Diversity%20in%20the%20High%20Tech%20Workforce%20and%20Sector%202014-2022.pdf

13. US EEOC, "High Tech, Low Inclusion."

14. US Bureau of Labor Statistics, "Employment in STEM Occupations," last modified August 29, 2024, https://www.bls.gov/emp/tables/stem-employment.htm.

15. McKinsey & Company, *Women in the Workplace 2024: The 10th-Anniversary Report*, September 17, 2024, https://www.mckinsey.com/featured-insights/diversity-and-inclusion/women-in-the-workplace; Webb, "60+ Women in Tech Statistics You Need to Know in 2025."

16. "State of Women in Tech and Startups 2023," Women Who Tech. Marie, *Survey Finds Sexism and Bias Still Major Issues for Women in Tech*, Web Summit, October 24, 2023, https://websummit.com/blog/news/women-tech-workplace-gender-bias-leadership-survey-report-2023/.

17. Kimberly Klayman, "What Female Founders Need to Know About Investment and Fundraising Trends," Technical.ly, August 30, 2024, https://technical.ly/diversity-equity-inclusion/female-founders-investment-trends-2024-ballard-spahr/.

18. Quek Jie Ann, "It's an 'Amazing Time' to Be a Woman in Business: Female Founders Say the Entrepreneurial Landscape Is Changing," CNBC, January 4, 2024, https://www.cnbc.com/2024/01/05/female-founders-say-it-is-an-amazing-time-for-women-to-be-in-business.html.

19. Dominic-Madori Davis, "Funding for Female Founders Remained Consistent in 2023," TechCrunch, January 10, 2024, https://techcrunch.com/2024/01/10/funding-for-female-founders-remained-consistent-in-2023/.

20. Donna Kelley et al., "Black Women Are More Likely to Start a Business than White Men," *Harvard Business Review*, May 11, 2021, https://hbr.org/2021/05/black-women-are-more-likely-to-start-a-business-than-white-men/.

21. "Sexual Harassment, Discrimination and Funding Disparities Rampant in Tech, Despite Promises for Progress—Latest Survey Reveals," Women Who Tech, December 12, 2023, https://womenwhotech.org/press/2023/12/sexual-harassment-discrimination-and-funding-disparities-rampant-tech-despite/.

22. "State of Women in Tech and Startups 2023," Women Who Tech.

23. Interview with female entrepreneur, March 20, 2025.

24. "State of Women in Tech and Startups 2023," Women Who Tech.

25. "Women Who Tech Startup & Tech Culture Survey 2020," Women Who Tech, September 2020, https://womenwhotech.org/sites/default/files/2020-09/WomenWho Tech_StartupAndTechSurvey2020.pdf

26. Issie Lapowsky, "This Is What Tech's Ugly Gender Problem Really Looks Like," *WIRED*, July 28, 2014, https://www.wired.com/2014/07/gender-gap/.

27. Tim Worstall, "This Part of Tech's Ugly Gender Problem Is Self-Solving," *Forbes*, July 30, 2014, https://www.forbes.com/sites/timworstall/2014/07/30/this-part-of-techs -ugly-gender-problem-is-self-solving/.

28. "8 Facts About Women in the Tech Industry," Women in Tech, March 29, 2023, https://www.womenintech.co.uk/8-facts-women-tech-industry/; "High Tech, Low Inclusion," U.S. Equal Employment Opportunity Commission, https://www.eeoc.gov /sites/default/files/2024-09/20240910_Diversity%20in%20the%20High%20Tech%20 Workforce%20and%20Sector%202014-2022.pdf/.

29. Kellogg School of Management, "Embracing the 'Socially Distinct' Outsider," News & Events, Northwestern University, April 7, 2009, https://www.kellogg.northwestern.edu /news_articles/2009/philipsresearch.aspx.

30. "Hacking Diversity with Inclusive Decision Making," Cloverpop, accessed April 21, 2024, https://www.cloverpop.com/hubfs/Whitepapers/Cloverpop_Hacking_Diversity _Inclusive_Decision_Making_White_Paper.pdf.

31. Erik Larson, "New Research: Diversity + Inclusion = Better Decision Making At Work," *Forbes*, September 21, 2017, https://www.forbes.com/sites/eriklarson/2017/09/21/new -research-diversity-inclusion-better-decision-making-at-work/.

Chapter 2

1. Mary Louise Kelly, "Silicon Valley's Ellen Pao Tackles Sex Discrimination, Workplace Diversity in Memoir," September 19, 2017, https://www.npr.org/sections/alltech considered/2017/09/19/551810814/silicon-valley-s-ellen-pao-tackles-sex-discrimination -workplace-diversity-in-mem/.

2. Elizabeth Weise, "Man Ellen Pao Accused of Retaliation Had Bonus Docked," *USA Today*, March 2, 2015, https://www.usatoday.com/story/tech/2015/03/02/ellen-pao -kleiner-perkins-ted-schlein-cocky/24267571/.

3. Colleen Taylor and Kim-Mai Cutler, "Ellen Pao 'Owns The Room,'" *TechCrunch*, March 9, 2015, https://techcrunch.com/2015/03/09/ellen-pao-owns-the-room/; Liz Gannes and Nellie Bowles, "Liveblog: Mary Meeker Testifies in Pao/Kleiner Perkins Case," Re/code, March 16, 2015, https://web.archive.org/web/20150914230431 /https://recode.net/2015/03/16/liveblog-mary-meeker-testifies-in-paokleiner-perkins

-case/; Mark Sullivan, "Ellen Pao Wanted Kleiner Perkins to Invest in Twitter in 2008. Kleiner Perkins Passed," VentureBeat, March 24, 2015, https://venturebeat.com/ business/ellen-pao-wanted-kleiner-perkins-to-invest-in-twitter-in-2008-kleiner -perkins-passed/.

4. Nellie Bowles and Liz Gannes, "All-Male Ski Trip and No Women at Al Gore Dinner: Kleiner's Chien Takes the Stand in Pao Lawsuit," Re/code, February 25, 2015, https ://web.archive.org/web/20151018233855/http://recode.net/2015/02/25/all-male-ski -trip-and-no-women-at-al-gore-dinner-kleiners-chien-takes-the-stand-in-pao-lawsuit/.

5. Bowles and Gannes, "All-Male Ski Trip."

6. Alexia Tsotsis, "Two Jurors on Opposite Sides Share Their Pao vs. Kleiner Perspectives," TechCrunch, March 27, 2015, https://techcrunch.com/2015/03/27/two-jurors-on -opposite-sides-share-their-pao-vs-kleiner-perspectives/.

7. Jessi Hempel, "The Pao Effect Is What Happens After Lean In," WIRED, September 20, 2017, https://www.wired.com/story/the-pao-effect-is-what-happens-after-lean-in/.

8. Margaret Cronin Fisk, "Next Up for Silicon Valley after Pao Loss: More Bias Suits," Bloomberg, March 28, 2015, https://www.bloomberg.com/news/articles/2015-03-28 /next-up-for-silicon-valley-after-pao-loss-more-bias-lawsuits/.

9. Issie Lapowsky, "Gender Bias Suit Will Soon Shine a Harsh Light on Microsoft," WIRED, September 18, 2015, https://www.wired.com/2015/09/microsoft-gender -lawsuit/; Julie Bort, "A Fed-Up Former Microsoft Employee Is Suing over Sex Discrimination," Business Insider India, September 16, 2015, https://www.business insider.in/A-fed-up-former-Microsoft-employee-is-suing-over-sex-discrimination /articleshow/48993650.cms.

10. Neil McAllister, "Hey Look! Microsoft's Workforce Isn't All White Men," The Register, January 4, 2015, https://www.theregister.com/2015/01/04/microsoft_diversity _numbers/.

11. Heather Kelly, "Facebook Gets Sued for Gender Discrimination," CNN Business, March 19, 2015, https://money.cnn.com/2015/03/18/technology/facebook -discrimination-suit/index.html.

12. "Class Certification Defeated in Twitter Gender Discrimination Case," SV Employment Law Firm, August 17, 2018, https://svelf.com/class-certification-defeated-in-twitter -gender-discrimination-case/.

13. Hayley Tsukayama, "The Network Effect at the Center of the Twitter Gender Discrimination Lawsuit," The Washington Post, March 23, 2015, https://www .washingtonpost.com/news/the-switch/wp/2015/03/23/the-network-effect-at-the -center-of-the-twitter-gender-discrimination-lawsuit/.

14. Christopher Davis, "Oracle Agrees to Settle Gender Discrimination Lawsuit," Working Solutions Law Firm, March 12, 2024, https://www.workingsolutionsnyc.com/blog /oracle-agrees-to-settle-gender-discrimination-lawsuit.

15. Katherine Long, "Oracle Women Fought 7 Years for Equity. Their Reward? An Extra Paycheck or 2," The Seattle Times, updated February 20, 2024, https://www.seattletimes

.com/business/oracle-women-fought-7-years-for-equity-their-reward-an-extra-paycheck
-or-2/.

16. Brendan Pierson, "Oracle to Settle Female Employees' Equal Pay Case for $25 Mln," Reuters, February 14, 2024, https://www.reuters.com/legal/litigation/oracle-settle -female-employees-equal-pay-case-25-mln-2024-02-14/.

17. Julie Bort and Taylor Nicole Rogers, "The Two Black Employees Who Took on Pinterest Explain Why They Quit, Their Fight for Pay, the Death Threats, the Private Investigator: 'It Was a Torturous Experience,'" *Business Insider*, June 24, 2020, https ://www.businessinsider.com/two-black-former-pinterest-employees-discuss-their-fight -for-pay-2020-6; Nitasha Tiku, "Black Women Say Pinterest Created a Den of Discrimination—Despite Its Image as the Nicest Company in Tech," *The Washington Post*, July 3, 2020, https://www.washingtonpost.com/technology/2020/07/03/pinterest -race-bias-black-employees/.

18. Daniel Wiessner, "Tesla Settles Race Bias Claims by Black Former Worker after $3 Million Verdict," Reuters, March 15, 2024, https://www.reuters.com/legal/tesla-settles -race-bias-claims-by-black-former-worker-2024-03-15/.

19. Jonathan Stempel, "Google Accused of Systemic Bias Against Black Employees in Recent Lawsuit," Reuters, March 18, 2022, https://www.reuters.com/business/media -telecom/google-is-accused-lawsuit-systemic-bias-against-black-employees-2022-03-18/.

20. Jessica Guynn, "Ellen Pao's Suit Was Wake-Up Call for Silicon Valley," *USA Today*, March 27, 2015, https://www.usatoday.com/story/tech/2015/03/27/ellen-pao-kleiner -perkins-verdict-silicon-valley/70557912/.

21. Colin Dwyer et al., "Women's March on Washington Goes Global: Postcards from Protests Around the World," The Two-Way, NPR, January 21, 2017, https://www.npr .org/sections/thetwo-way/2017/01/21/510940708/womens-march-on-washington -goes-worldwide-snapshots-from-around-the-globe/.

22. Nicole Murphy, "Types of Bias," CPD Online College, updated January 15, 2025, https://cpdonline.co.uk/knowledge-base/safeguarding/types-of-bias.

23. Murphy, "Types of Bias."

24. European Institute for Gender Equality, "What Is Sexism?" in *Sexism at Work: How Can We Stop It?*, Part 1: Understand, accessed April 24, 2024, https://eige.europa.eu /publications-resources/toolkits-guides/sexism-at-work-handbook/part-1-understand /what-sexism?language_content_entity=en.; Imogen Calderwood and Erica Sánchez, "There's Finally an Internationally Agreed Upon Definition of Sexism. Here's Why That Matters," Global Citizen, April 1, 2019, https://www.globalcitizen.org/en/content /sexism-definition-council-of-europe-equality/.

25. "Sexual Harassment Laws in Employment," Justia Employment Law Center, last reviewed October 2024, https://www.justia.com/employment/employment -discrimination/sexual-harassment/.

26. US Equal Employment Opportunity Commission, "Sexual Harassment," accessed April 24, 2024, https://www.eeoc.gov/sexual-harassment.

27. World Health Organization, "Ageing: Ageism," March 18, 2021, https://www.who.int /news-room/questions-and-answers/item/ageing-ageism.

28. Google, "Racism," accessed April 21, 2024, https://www.google.com/search ?q=definition+of+racism; Wikipedia, "Racism," last modified April 3, 2025, https ://en.wikipedia.org/wiki/Racism.

29. Wikipedia, "Microaggression," last modified April 6, 2025, https://en.wikipedia.org /wiki/Microaggression.

Chapter 3

1. European Institute for Gender Equality, "Where Does Sexism Come From?" in *Sexism at Work: How Can We Stop It?*, Part 1: Understand, accessed May 14, 2024, https://eige .europa.eu/publications-resources/toolkits-guides/sexism-at-work-handbook/part-1 -understand/where-does-sexism-come?language_content_entity=en.

2. Jamie Newton, "The Gender Credibility Gap (That's What She Said)," TEDxMileHigh, accessed May 14, 2024, https://www.tedxmilehigh.com/gender-credibility-gap/.

3. Professor Nicole Gugliucci (@NoisyAstronomer), "My friends coined a word: hepeated. For when a woman suggests an idea and it's ignored, but then a guy says same thing and everyone loves it," Twitter (now X) September 22, 2017, https://x.com/noisy astronomer/status/911213826527436800?lang=en.

4. Fran Hauser, "Advice from a Nice Girl: How Do I Take Back Credit for My Idea?" Refinery29, March 25, 2019, https://www.refinery29.com/en-us/what-is-hepeating -speaking-up-in-meetings; Lindsay Dodgson, "Men Are Getting the Credit for Women's Work through Something Called 'Hepeating'—Here's What It Means," *Business Insider*, March 8, 2018, https://www.businessinsider.com/what-is-hepeating-2017-9.

5. John D'Amelio, "Taylor Swift on 'Lover' and Haters," Sunday Morning, CBS News, updated August 25, 2019, https://www.cbsnews.com/news/taylor-swift-on-lover-and -haters/.

6. Yessi Bello Perez, "Sick of Sexism in Tech? Share This Article Next Time You're Pissed Off," The Next Web, March 8, 2020, https://thenextweb.com/news/sick-of-sexism-in -tech-share-this-article-next-time-youre-pissed-off/.

7. Rakesh Kochhar, "The Enduring Grip of the Gender Pay Gap," Pew Research Center, March 1, 2023, https://www.pewresearch.org/social-trends/2023/03/01/the-enduring -grip-of-the-gender-pay-gap/; Emma Woollacott, "Male Workers Say Sexism in the Tech Industry Is 'Rare'—Women Would Disagree," ITPro, February 15, 2024, https://www .itpro.com/business/business-strategy/male-workers-say-sexism-in-the-tech-industry-is -rare-women-would-disagree/.

8. Kochhar, "Enduring Grip of the Gender Pay Gap"; Woollacott, "Male Workers Say Sexism in the Tech Industry."

9. American Association of University Women, *The Simple Truth About the Gender Pay Gap* (Washington, DC: AAUW, 2025), https://www.aauw.org/resources/research/simple-truth/.

10. Corinne Post, "Golf-Loving CEOs May Pose Gender Discrimination Risk for Companies," *Forbes*, May 10, 2023, https://www.forbes.com/sites/corinnepost/2023/05/10/golf-loving-ceos-may-pose-gender-discrimination-risk-for-companies/.

Chapter 4

1. Liam Soutar, "Google-Owned Firm Sparks Outrage after 'Ignoring' Sexual Assault Claims," HR Grapevine, May 10, 2022, https://www.hrgrapevine.com/us/content/article/2022-04-06-google-owned-firm-sparks-outrage-after-ignoring-sexual-assault-claims/.

2. Madhumita Murgia, "DeepMind Accused of Mishandling Sexual Misconduct Allegations," *Financial Times*, March 30, 2022, https://www.ft.com/content/928c5a91-baaa-41f2-b922-a07c74704e47/.

3. Interview with Erica [pseud.], May 18, 2024.

4. Interview with Madeline [pseud.], May 15, 2024.

5. Catherine Mattice, "Why It's Getting Harder for Some Women to Report Harassment," LinkedIn, March 20, 2024, https://www.linkedin.com/pulse/why-its-getting-harder-some-women-report-harassment-catherine-0sy9c/.

6. Interview with Kristine [pseud.], May 18, 2024.

7. Interview with Kristine [pseud.].

Chapter 5

1. Tricia Lucas, "Blatant Ageism in Tech: Why You Should Hire Employees over 50," LinkedIn, September 27, 2016, https://www.linkedin.com/pulse/blatant-ageism-tech-why-you-should-hire-employees-over-lucas-mba/.

2. Lucas, "Blatant Ageism in Tech."

3. Lawrence R. Samuel, "Young People Are Just Smarter," Aging, *Psychology Today*, October 2, 2017, https://www.psychologytoday.com/us/blog/boomers-30/201710/young-people-are-just-smarter/.

4. Sheila Callaham, "LinkedIn under Fire for Ageist Ads: Fails to Take Timely Action and Uphold DEI Policy," *Forbes*, March 8, 2024, https://www.forbes.com/sites/sheilacallaham/2024/03/08/linkedin-under-fire-for-ageist-ads-fails-to-take-timely-action-and-uphold-dei-policy/.

5. Matthew Gooding, "IBM Settles 'Dinobabies' Age Discrimination Case," *Tech Monitor*, August 17, 2022, https://www.techmonitor.ai/leadership/workforce/ibm-dinobabies-age-discrimination-case/.

6. Stacy Thomas, "HR Leaders Suing IBM for 'Blatant' Ageism," HRD America, October 3, 2023, https://www.hcamag.com/us/news/general/hr-leaders-suing-ibm-for-blatant-ageism/461778/.

7. "IBM Must Face Ex-Workers' Age Bias Suit," Cohen Milstein, March 28, 2024, https://www.cohenmilstein.com/ibm-must-face-ex-workers-age-bias-suit/.

8. Peter Gosselin and Ariana Tobin, "Amid Accusations of Age Bias, IBM Winds Down a Push for Millennial Workers," *ProPublica*, September 19, 2018, https://www.propublica.org/article/amid-accusations-of-age-bias-ibm-winds-down-a-push-for-millennial-workers/.

9. "5 Ways to Prove Age-Based Discrimination in the Workplace," *Workplace Discrimination* (blog), Wenzel Fenton Cabassa, PA, accessed May 30, 2024, https://www.wenzelfenton.com/blog/2024/02/08/ways-to-prove-age-based-discrimination-in-the-workplace/.

10. Kimberly Palmer, "10 Things You Should Know About Age Discrimination," *AARP*, updated October 31, 2024, https://www.aarp.org/work/age-discrimination/facts-in-the-workplace/.

11. "5 Ways to Prove Age-Based Discrimination."

12. "How to Prove Age Discrimination at Work," Employee Rights Attorney Group, accessed May 30, 2024, https://www.employeerightsattorneygroup.com/employment-law/discrimination/age-discrimination/proving-age-discrimination/.

Chapter 6

1. Interview with Tracy [pseud.], March 5, 2025.

2. Interview with Nicki [pseud.], June 26, 2024.

3. US Department of Justice, "Laws We Enforce," Civil Rights Division, updated February 12, 2025, https://www.justice.gov/crt/laws-we-enforce.

Chapter 7

1. Malissa Alinor, "Research: The Real-Time Impact of Microaggressions," *Harvard Business Review*, May 17, 2022, https://hbr.org/2022/05/research-the-real-time-impact-of-microaggressions/.

2. Jillesa Gebhardt, "Study: Microaggressions in the Workplace," SurveyMonkey, accessed June 26, 2024, https://www.surveymonkey.com/curiosity/microaggressions-research/.

3. Interview with Tamara [pseud.], June 28, 2024.

4. "The Official Campaign of the CROWN Act Led by the CROWN Coalition," CROWN Coalition, Dove, accessed June 26, 2024, https://www.thecrownact.com/.

5. "The Official Campaign."

6. "The Official Campaign."

7. Interview with Elena [pseud.], June 26, 2024.

8. Rob Wile and Char Adams, "'Black Jobs'? Trump Draws Pushback after Anti-Immigration Rant," NBC News, June 28, 2024, https://www.nbcnews.com/news/nbcblk/trumps-anti-immigration-black-jobs-reactions-presidential-debate-rcna159375/.

9. Savannah James-Bayly, "Microaggressions: How and Why Do They Impact Health?" *Medical News Today*, May 2, 2022, https://www.medicalnewstoday.com/articles/microaggressions-how-and-why-do-they-impact-health/.

10. Alinor, "Real-Time Impact of Microaggressions."

Chapter 8

1. Clive Boddy, "Psychopathic Leadership A Case Study of a Corporate Psychopath CEO," *Journal of Business Ethics* vol. 145, pg. 141–156, October 19, 2015, https://doi.org/10.1007/s10551-015-2908-6.

2. Ross Pomeroy, "How Many 'Corporate Psychopaths' Are CEOs?" *Big Think*, May 26, 2023, https://bigthink.com/leadership/corporate-psychopath-ceo/.

3. Lars Kimmig, "Beneath the Surface—How Dark Personality Traits of CEOs Influence Top Management Team Formation," *Academy of Management Proceedings* 2024, no. 1 (2024), https://doi.org/10.5465/AMPROC.2024.17011abstract; Peter Willis, "How to Deal with the Dark Triad (Psychopaths, Narcissists, Machiavels) While Avoiding Unethical Office Politics," Unchain Your Brain, August 11, 2024, https://www.unchainyourbrain.org/2024/08/11/how-to-deal-with-the-dark-triad-psychopaths-narcissists-machiavels-while-avoiding-unethical-office-politics/.

4. Mayo Clinic, "Narcissistic Personality Disorder—Symptoms and Causes," April 6, 2023, https://www.mayoclinic.org/diseases-conditions/narcissistic-personality-disorder/symptoms-causes/syc-20366662/.

5. Interview with Derek [pseud.], June 19, 2024.

6. Andrea Petrone, "The Warning Signs of Egocentric Leaders," LinkedIn, June 11, 2022, https://www.linkedin.com/pulse/warning-signs-egocentric-leaders-andrea-petrone-1e/.

About the Author

KAE KRONTHALER-WILLIAMS is a global marketing executive in the software industry and a passionate advocate for women's advancement in the workplace. She uses her platform to confront bias, challenge toxic work cultures, and spark change through writing, public speaking, coaching, and nonprofit work. Her mission: Ensure every woman is seen, supported, and empowered to lead.

www.ingramcontent.com/pod-product-compliance
Lightning Source LLC
Chambersburg PA
CBHW030507210326
41597CB00013B/831